from award-winning author

Lisa Wysocky

fura books

Published by
Fura Books
P.O. Box 90751
Nashville, TN 37209

The Library of Congress Cataloging-in-Publication Data Applied For
Lisa Wysocky—
Therapy Horse Selection: A My Horse, My Partner Book
p. cm
ISBN-1-890224-09-7
1. Horses 2. Horse Training 3. Alternative Therapies
I. Title
2014

Printed in the United States of America

3 5 7 9 10 8 6 4 2

For interviews, bulk purchases, or other information please contact
lisainfo@comcast.net, www.LisaWysocky.com

The information in this book is meant to supplement, not replace, education and training about horses and equine assisted activities and therapies. Any activity involving horses poses some inherent risk. The author and publisher advise readers to take full responsibility for their safety and know their limits. Before practicing the skills described in this book, be sure that any equipment you use is well maintained, and do not take risks beyond your level of experience, aptitude, training, and comfort level.

Dedication

To therapy horses everywhere.
Thank you for your many talents and gifts.

Dear Readers,

Therapy Horse Selection is something the therapeutic riding industry has needed for a long time. As a TR professional for many years, I realize there is no perfect horse, and that the many variables of each horse should all be a part of the puzzle. This very informative read helps us see the many pieces, and explains why and how they fit together.

Lisa Wysocky has a great way of describing with words and uses a lot of real-life visuals that are truly useful. Examples and situations that people will encounter out in the field are hard to capture, but she does it with ease. She also doesn't assume readers already have common knowledge, yet moves through topics without boring more advanced readers.

This book does a great job educating center staff who are looking for the right horse, as well as the rest of the horse community about what is important and why. Many people think their horse is "retiring" when entering the therapy world, because they think the physical work is less than in the competitive world. I've often heard, "Why would I donate my horse? He isn't lame or old enough to give away." This book is the answer to that question.

This is certainly a book that our center will have in our library and refer to often! I highly recommend *Therapy Horse Selection* to people interested in the therapy horse: center staff, prospective donors, trainers, instructors, board members, and volunteers who want to understand more about the process of horse selection.

Mary Mitten, executive director
We Can Ride, Minnetonka, Minnesota, wecanride.org
PATH Intl. Advanced Instructor

Table of Contents

Additional Books by Lisa Wysocky

Nonfiction

The Power of Horses: True Stories from Country Music Stars

Success Within: How to Create the Greatest Moments of Your Life

Front of the Class: How Tourette Syndrome Made Me the Teacher I Never Had (with Brad Cohen)

My Horse, My Partner: Teamwork on the Ground (also available in DVD format)

Horse Country: A Celebration of Country Music and the Love of Horses

Two Foot Fred: How My Life Has Come Full Circle (with Fred Gill)

Success Talks: 101 Positive Things to Say to Yourself

Walking on Eggshells: Discovering Strength and Courage Amid Chaos (with Lyssa Chapman)

Horseback: A Memoir of My Early Years with Horses

Hidden Girl: The True Story of A Modern-Day Child Slave (with Shyima Hall)

Fiction

The Opium Equation: A Cat Enright Equestrian Mystery

The Magnum Equation: A Cat Enright Equestrian Mystery

Introduction

I am continually amazed at the talents of therapy horses. Every day they tolerate loud children, sidewalkers who dig elbows into their sides, and multiple handlers who do not have time to bond with them or establish leadership. Every day these horses step up to make a difference in the lives of humans—and not just program participants. Therapy horses make a positive difference in the lives of staff, instructors, volunteers, parents, and caregivers, too.

Most of you who have picked up this book might already be involved in the field of equine assisted activities: therapy, mental health, or learning. Some of you might be new into this journey, while others have been here for decades. You might also be interested because you have a horse you'd like to donate to a center. Or, you tried to donate a horse and did not understand why the horse was rejected. The following chapters will address all of that, and more. I am most thrilled, however, that you felt a need to make a difference in your own unique way.

Your passion might be through PATH (Professional Association of Therapeutic Horsemanship), EAGALA (Equine Assisted Growth and Learning Association), E3A (Equine Experiential Education Association), AHA (American Hippotherapy Association), or another great organization. Your interest could be in therapeutic riding, driving, ground activities, vaulting, or even able-bodied horsemanship. Whatever your interest, the following pages outline the process I use when looking for a new horse either for a therapeutic riding center or for an individual. In looking for a horse for a specific person, some of the paperwork discussed may not be needed, otherwise, the process (including teamwork) is applicable for any horse you might look for.

Like many of you, I began my journey into this field as a volunteer. I went on to become the equine trainer at a large center in Tennessee, and then became certified as a PATH instructor. This was after being an able-bodied riding instructor for more than thirty-five years and earning a degree in equine management from the University of Minnesota. After I began speaking at state, regional, and international PATH conferences, I was invited to do trainings for staff, horses, and volunteers at many centers. There, I found unique differences and astounding sameness at centers across the United States.

For example, different geographic locations present special challenges to many programs. Those located in colder climates that do not run all year often have difficulty getting their horse's minds focused at the start of the new program year in the spring. Southern centers have more trouble with heat related stresses with their horses, and for many centers on the West Coast, pasture and turnout are at a premium.

On the other hand, many programs, no matter where they are, have difficulty finding that perfect "big" horse, or a safe canter horse for their advanced participants. Most program directors jump for joy just to find a horse who is sound, or one that is under twenty years of age. Equine burnout is a common theme, as is soreness.

I have had the extreme honor and privilege to be closely involved with many therapy horses at a number of centers. And while I use the term "horse" throughout most of this book, I use it as an encompassing term. All equines share wondrous gifts. Whether donkey, miniature- or draft mule, hinny, or any other equine, many programs have all kinds in their herd.

One day I saw a retired foxhunter, an absolute pistol when an able-bodied person rode him, relax and turn into a babysitter when a rider with a disability was near. A fabulous independent walk/trot horse, this gelding developed his riders into more than any instructor thought possible.

In 2005 I was presented a unique challenge: take a three-year-old rescue horse who had been abandoned as a yearling, and who wasn't really halter broke, and turn him into a therapy horse. On the plus side, he was 14.2, narrow, extremely intelligent, and had a cadenced walk that gave the rider a lot of pelvic movement. On the down side, he did not know how to relate to either horses or humans and spent his first months at a center in Tennessee in a paddock near the barn watching horse/horse, horse/human, and human/human interactions. Long story short, six years later Valentino was chosen as the 2011 PATH International Equine of the Year. To my knowledge, he is the only horse specifically trained for equine assisted activities and therapies to be awarded this prestigious honor.

In my experience, the most successful therapy horses, the horses who are the most helpful to centers, the mares and geldings who stay in programs the longest, are the ones who are there by careful selection, rather than by chance. These are the horses who passed pre-donation vet exams with flying colors, whose good conformation keeps them sound, and whose "horse sense" gives them the ability to intuit exactly what a program participant needs from them.

But how, exactly, do you find horses like that? And how do you know at first glance whether or not an individual horse has a good chance at becoming a star at your center? Those are the questions we will explore over the next eighteen chapters—along with answers, options, and ideas to bring the quality of your herd to a higher level.

My goal is to give you the tools; it is up to you to use them.

Lisa Wysocky
June 2014

PART I

Your Equine Committee 1

Often, the responsibility of finding new horses falls to one person, but several eyes, brains, and hearts are much better suited to make an informed decision of that magnitude. If you are part of a therapeutic center, your equine committee is the first step in finding your perfect therapy horse. If you are an individual who is looking for a horse, think of your trainer, instructor, family, and friends as your committee. At a center your committee could include the equine manager, lead instructor, program manager, and a trusted volunteer. In some cases, all of these positions involve just one person!

The advantages of an equine committee are many. First, it takes the "heat" off a single individual. Let's say, for example, that your current board treasurer offers your center a twelve-year-old retired reining horse. Let's also say that your equine manager and your board treasurer sometimes have differences of opinion. And just to make it fun, we will assume that your board treasurer is also your biggest donor.

The horse seems perfect, but once you get her on property you find that she has a habit of bucking, just a little, when she is first ridden. If the equine manager feels that this horse is a safety risk and wants to send the horse home, it could look like the manager doesn't want the horse because of the dynamic she has with the donor.

An equine committee, however, neutralizes that—and other—awkward moments. If the committee tells the board treasurer that the horse is not suitable, it is perceived as less personal than if one person made the decision.

Second, the theory that two heads are better than one is true. It's also true that four heads are better than two. In looking at prospective horses one person's eyes might catch a lameness that another person misses. One person's preference for wide, quarter-type horses can be balanced by another's feel for the narrower Walking Horse or Arabian. And don't forget brainstorming as a problem-solving tool. In this way, the best needs of the program are met—as long as you have the right people on the committee.

So just who is on an equine committee? In many cases the job determines some of the committee members. Centers often include their equine person, lead instructor, and program director, and these people stay on the committee as long as they hold the job. The rest of the committee is made up of two to four others who are actively involved in the center. These members could be instructors or volunteers, but need to be experienced horsemen or horsewomen who also understand the needs of the program. These "extra" people typically serve terms of two to three years, and then rotate off so other people have the opportunity to participate.

APPOINTMENT OR APPLICATION?

Staff at your center will have to determine whether the non-job related members of your equine committee are appointed, or if they have to apply. There are pros and cons with both methods. If a committee member is appointed, you often get the cream of the crop, but it can be at the disgruntled disappointment of others. Of course the appointed member has to agree to serve, but someone who is passed over could feel that the committee is a "clique," or that you have to belong to an "in" crowd at your center to get on the committee.

The application method is far more democratic, as people who have the most to offer are usually chosen. If a person is disappointed at being passed over, there is written documentation about why the choice was made. The problem lies in the fact that oftentimes the people you'd really like to have on the committee don't apply. For those who are interested, there is a sample equine committee application in Appendix A (page 135).

There is no perfect answer to the question of appointment versus application. But, a meeting of your center's decision makers should be able to set up a process that works for your center, especially when they keep in mind that the equine committee is often responsible for far more than just looking at prospective horses. Your committee can also be in charge of everything from saddle fitting to deciding rider weight limits for individual horses. The committee can help determine medical direction for horses who are ill or injured, mandate the number of lessons a horse will be part of every week, make policy and procedure recommendations, and even help find good homes for horses who retire from your program. While the specific duties of an equine committee vary from center to center, the constant is the united front the committee presents to the betterment of your program.

In selecting new horses for your center, it is best if several people from the committee can look at the prospective horse. One center I consult for has a very knowledgeable equine committee member who doesn't like gray or white horses. If decisions about incoming horses were left solely to him, this center would have missed out on several of their top therapy horses. However, he brings a lot to the table when it comes to analyzing a horse's gait and movement, so is a valued member of the team.

Having several committee members also takes the pressure off one person when it comes to scheduling. If the equine manager is busy because four horses have suddenly developed odd behaviors in lessons, then several other committee members can go instead. With video cameras on most cell phones, it is easy to film the visit for other committee members to view later, if necessary.

But before any of that happens someone has to decide what kind of horses you need, and what you need them to do.

Determining Need 2

Before you can look at horses for yourself or your program, you need to know what kind of horses will be most beneficial. If, for example, most of your program participants take part in unmounted activities, you will have a different herd than programs that mostly have mounted riders. Programs that offer hippotherapy, vaulting, and/or driving in addition to riding will need yet another kind of herd. This is just one instance where your equine committee becomes invaluable. The committee can work with the program head and lead instructor to determine both existing and upcoming needs.

A few years ago, in a review of rider profiles, one program I work with discovered they had a number of boys in the thirteen- to fourteen-year-old age range. The program staff was astute enough to realize that very shortly these boys would undergo a major growth spurt and, while the program's herd currently worked well, in six months to a year the program was going to need several more horses who could carry taller and heavier riders. They immediately put the word out among supporters and had the horses in place, trained, and ready to go when they needed them.

If this center had not acted with so much foresight one of two things would have happened. First, the boys might have been mounted on horses who were too short for them, or on horses who ideally should not have been carrying the weight of these now much larger boys. In these scenarios you risk soreness and behavior problems in your horse herd, and may eventually have to take a horse out of lessons—either temporarily or permanently.

The second scenario involves telling the boys' parents or caregivers that you do not have a horse for them, and no one ever wants to have that conversation. No one wants to tell an existing participant that they can no longer ride, and while many programs do have alternative activities they can plug the rider into (such as stable management or therapeutic driving) many centers do not have this luxury.

To avoid either of these possibilities, let's look at some specific characteristics of horses you might need for your program. We will discuss these traits, along with many others, in depth in later chapters, but this will give you a starting overview.

SIZE

Based on the population of your participants right now, and also a year from now, do you need a 13 hand pony for the many younger riders that you have, or do you need a 15.2 hand babysitter to carry larger, more independent, riders?

WIDTH

Width is critical if you serve a population of riders with physical disabilities. Those with cerebral palsy (CP) especially need a narrower horse, as do some Down syndrome riders who have shorter legs. However, depending on the rider's balance and center of gravity, other riders with Down syndrome, for example, could better benefit from a horse of medium, or even wide width.

SOUNDNESS

Every center needs a horse who is 100 percent sound, right? Not necessarily. Centers that do a lot of unmounted work could give a wonderful job and home to a horse who is "serviceably" sound. If you do unmounted equine assisted learning or psychotherapy, your otherwise perfect horse may have a bowed tendon or some ringbone (osteoarthritis in the pastern) that makes the horse unsuitable for mounted activities. But, the horse's personality and other characteristics might make him or her invaluable for unmounted activities.

GAIT AND MOVEMENT

What kind of movement do you need to fill the gap in your herd? Do you need a horse with smooth gaits for physically fragile riders? Or, will a horse with a ground-pounding trot help your autistic riders focus? At the walk, should the horse move the rider's pelvis in a forward to back motion, side to side, or a figure eight?

AGE

Most centers have guidelines for the age range of horses who are accepted as part of the program. While not set in stone, most programs set incoming age ranges somewhere between eight and eighteen. However, each day every member of the herd becomes one day older. If the horses in your herd are mostly in their twenties—or thirties—and nearing retirement, then you may want to give preference to incoming horses who are on the younger spectrum of your age range.

TRAINING

When I first began to select horses for equine assisted activities and therapies, a board member at one center cautioned me that his center didn't need any horse who had high level or special training. The typical "whoa and go" trail horse was fine for his center. I was appalled.

While a horse with a "grade school" education can work well in EAAT (equine assisted activities and therapies), what about riders who have progressed beyond the knowledge of a horse with a limited education? In determining what kind of training prospective horses for your program need, remember to consider your more advanced riders. In addition, horses who are trained to move off a rider's leg can build a lot of confidence in a rider who has a partial leg paralysis or in a rider with CP.

TEMPERAMENT

The words kind, giving, sensible, and steady all come to mind when you think of a therapy horse, but not every horse needs to be "push-button," or a push over. Some riders benefit from a horse who presents a challenge. Over a year's time, I watched one timid young woman progress by leaps and bounds when she was paired with the pushiest horse in the herd. He taught her to focus and step up her game, and while the relationship was a struggle at first, today they are best friends.

In short, every center needs a variety of horse sizes and shapes, training and temperaments. One center I know of originally had all Tennessee Walking Horses. While the executive director's love for the breed was admirable, even he soon found that one breed could not possibly best serve all of their riders.

Appendix B (page 136) is a chart that will help you discover the needs of your riders, and in Appendix C (page 137), there is a form that will help you assess your existing horse herd. If you compare the two forms, you will be able to see what specific gaps need to be filled in your herd.

Depending on the size of your program, and whether you are open seasonally or throughout the year, someone from your center should update these two forms annually. Busier programs can benefit from updates every six months.

Some programs put a list of qualifications on their website that new horses coming into the program need to meet. This lets potential donors know right away if their horse is suitable. You can quickly modify criteria as needed, or put a notice that you are, for example, especially looking for a 13 hand to 13.2 hand narrow pony. Your qualifications might look something like:

To be accepted for our ninety-day trial, your horse must meet the following:

Be a mare or gelding between age seven and eighteen

If a mare, she must not be pregnant, or have had a foal within the past eight months

Be no less than 11 hands (or 44 inches) and no more than 16.1 hands (65 inches) at the wither

If taller than thirteen hands, able to walk, trot (or gait), and canter with a rider

Be sound, with little to no physical limitation

Respond well to voice and leg signals

Be well-mannered on the ground

Be accepting of unusual situations

Be respectful of many different handlers and experiences

Fill a need in our program, as determined by our equine committee

Once here, to be accepted permanently into our program your horse must also meet the following requirements:

Pass examinations performed by our veterinarian and farrier with no major concerns

Pass 85 percent of all staff evaluations

Pass 85 percent of our equine committee's evaluations

Horse Donation Profile 3

The horse donation profile is a form that is filled out by the horse donor, or seller. It details the characteristics of a prospective horse, and also gives background and veterinary information. Many centers keep their horse donation profile form on their website as a downloadable Word document or PDF file that can be completed by a horse owner, then mailed, emailed, or faxed to the center.

The form is a handy tool that allows the center's equine team to choose which horses they want to take a look at, and which they can easily see are not suitable. The questions that are asked on the form can also be updated regularly, according to the needs of the center.

Another plus is that the profile gives your equine committee concrete reasons why a horse is *not* suitable for your program. If a prospective horse is a cribber (a horse who grabs onto surfaces such as fence boards with her teeth and sucks in air) and you do not have the resources to replace damaged fences or provide veterinary care for the horse's worn-down teeth or other health problems caused by the cribbing, then you can educate the horse owner as to why you have passed on the kind offer of her horse.

Educate, by the way, is the key word. Many horse owners become disappointed and angry if their horse is not accepted into a program. They truly believe their horse would make a perfect therapy horse, but they do not understand the needs of the program—or of the field in general. Others really do believe a center is the perfect place to offload a problem, old, unhealthy, or unsound horse. When they are told no, they become disgruntled.

One way around this is to invite the prospective donor to your center for a visit. Once they see what horses are asked to do both physically and emotionally, many people begin to understand the wonder of the therapy horse. Not everyone gets it, but some do.

YOUR HORSE DONATION PROFILE FORM

What you include on your form will be specific to the nature of your program. Some ideas are included here, as well as in Appendix D (page 138).

CONTACT INFORMATION

As much of this as you can get is always helpful. The donor's name, address, phone, email, and the physical location of the horse should all be included.

BASICS ABOUT THE HORSE

You may be able to eliminate the horse on the basis of weight, height, age, color, breed, build, or sex. If you have a lot of big horses but desperately need a narrow 12 hand pony, you may not be as interested in looking at a bulky 16 hand Quarter Horse, especially if the horse is in her twenties. On the other hand, many owners misjudge these aspects of their horses. One horse I looked at for an individual rider was purported to be 17 hands, but I arrived to find she was a solid 15.2.

Other items that should be on this section of the donation profile include information on white markings, scars, temperament, training, and past competition or trail experience. Anytime a horse is exposed to the world outside his or her pasture fence, it builds (hopefully) safe reference points, and those horses often do well in making a transition to a therapy center. If, however, the horse competed in dressage, reining, polo, barrel racing, or any other demanding sport for a long period of time, there may be soundness issues. Just as an old football player may gimp around, so might an older competition horse.

THE HORSE'S HEALTH

This is the section where many horse owners tend to "fudge." Questions such as has the horse ever foundered, colicked, or choked are sometimes "overlooked." Other questions, such as the date of the horse's last physical, worming, or farrier or trimmer visit puts some prospective donors off—if the visits have not been recent. Does the horse crib or weave? Has she been diagnosed with Navicular disease or allergies? Have the horse's hocks ever been injected? Is she up to date on coggins and vaccinations? Is the horse dominant or submissive in the pasture? Hard to catch? On medication? Does she need special shoeing? Interestingly enough, some owners can't imagine why you want all this information.

Depending on your program, the answers to most of these questions, no matter what they are, should not automatically eliminate the horse from consideration, but too many red flags poking up in the field of answers could make you hesitant to move forward.

Is it also a good idea to ask the donor to call the horse's veterinarian and have the horse's medical records released to you. If the owner won't do that, he or she might be trying to hide a problem. If the owner does not have a veterinarian who looks in on the horse—at least on an annual basis—that could be a problem, too.

THE HORSE'S TRAINING

The horse's education is also important and should be noted on the donation profile. While a horse who just knows "go and whoa" might be a training challenge, so might a sensitive third level dressage horse. However, I have worked with and seen many awesome therapy horses of both extremes.

Your donation profile should ask whether or not the horse knows how to longe, load into and out of a trailer, cross tie (or tie at all), ground drive, and pull a cart or buggy. It is also good to know if the horse canters easily, knows lead cues, side- or halfpasses, backs easily, and collects and extends. Again, this is not information either way that should exclude the horse from your program. Rather, it is a diagnostic tool to determine where the horse might best fit within your center.

PHOTOS

You can ask for a good side view photo of the horse, one that shows the horse's conformation and markings on all four legs. Head shots and front and rear shots of the horse standing squarely are good to have, too. Owners, however, sometimes do not have that, or are not good photographers. Sometimes weather interferes with them shooting new photos, especially in winter in northern climates. Poor lighting and bad angles also keep you from getting a good idea of the horse, as do photos of the horse tacked or performing whatever they did in their previous job. It is nice, though, to get two or three photos of the horse with the donation profile, whatever the quality or view.

SUMMARY

Finally, a good summary question to ask is why the owner wants to donate (or lease) the horse to your center. Why does he or she feel the horse will be a good fit? This last question will give additional insight into all of the pros and cons about the horse, because just as there is no perfect person, there is no perfect horse. Many come close, however, and the donation profile will help you find those horses who do.

Horse Assessment Form 4

The horse assessment form is different from the horse donation profile, as it is an internal document. The horse donation profile should either be on your center's website, or available via email on request. The assessment form, however, is a document that is developed by your equine team, and is used to assess or evaluate prospective horses when you visit them for the first time. There is a sample form in Appendix E (page 139). You may also be interested in a quick, ten-minute assessment process, found in Appendix F (page 141).

The form has a secondary use, as well. It can also be used to evaluate existing horses in your program. As your horses age, or if one becomes unhappy, the form can be used to help determine if the horse is still suitable for your needs. As the field of therapeutic riding, equine assisted learning, and all the many other different ways that horses help people expands, you may find that your program changes, too. That means your equine needs will change along with everything else.

ADDITIONAL BENEFITS

The horse assessment form is great to use in conjunction with the horse donation profile. But instead of the owner's wonderful claims about the horse, here you can record your own observations. Not every horse owner is dishonest. Far from it. But, there are a small number who are. Or, the owner is well-meaning but uneducated about horses and horse care—and about the field of equine therapies and activities.

Another benefit of the form is that everyone who goes out to look at the horse can fill in their own copy with their individual impressions to create a written record of the horse on the day you visit. If you choose to pass on the horse, you now have concrete reasons, versus unspecified, undocumented grounds that are more subjective. Concrete facts often keep the horse's owner from having hard feelings and being disappointed.

WHAT TO INCLUDE

Horse size, breed, sex, color, build, and markings will have been on the horse donation profile, but you can make your own observations on the assessment form. Remember that the owner or donor may not have given accurate information. In addition, you can assess temperament, demeanor, posture, soreness, gait, whether or not the horse is comfortable with sidewalkers, and if unusual objects such as nerf balls, plastic, bells, etcetera, bother him. Depending on the focus and needs of your program, you can add assessment categories to include activities such as driving or vaulting, or delete as needed.

It also helps if, in addition to your comments, you rate the horse in each category on a scale of one to five. That helps anyone who did not go with you to visit the horse get a better understanding of the horse's strengths and weaknesses.

If, say, the horse was tense around sidewalkers, one person might comment "a little nervous," while another might say, "didn't like sidewalkers," or "accepted sidewalkers after a few minutes." Individually, those three statements can mean many things. As a whole, you get the impression that the horse needed work in this area. If, however, all three people who visited the horse scored her as a "3," a score that is indicative of average, it sheds more light.

Another benefit is that if you look at a number of horses on the same day, or over a few days, the horses tend to get jumbled in your mind. Was it the bay mare who had so much rotational movement at the walk, or was it the chestnut gelding? The assessment form keeps all the facts about each horse in a clear and orderly manner.

A full assessment can take an hour or more, if you are thorough. You might find, though, that you've seen enough after fifteen or twenty minutes. Actually, you sometimes know you are going to pass after the first five minutes, or even after catching a glimpse of the horse from the other side of the pasture. But, out of consideration to the owner, you should take time to look closer. These situations can offer many teachable moments for newer members of your team, and for the rest of the team, too. Plus, it allows you to educate the owner about your program, and that person may become a volunteer or donate another, more suitable, horse in the future.

Also, if you see that the horse is neglected or abused, a closer look will offer you two important opportunities. The first is to gently teach the horse owner about proper treatment, nutrition, care, and safety hazards that might be seen in the pasture. The second is to have more information to give to county authorities or your local rescue organization—if you feel that is a route you need to go. Unfortunately, not every horse owner is knowledgeable and caring about horses.

LATER USE

If you bring the horse in for a ninety-day trial (more on this later) the assessment form can come in handy months later. If sixty days in the horse is not quite where you hoped she would be, it is helpful to go back to the assessment form to see everyone's initial thoughts. So often first impressions are spot on. That's why it is important to keep each completed horse assessment in the horse's folder, or wherever your equine records are kept. You never know when the information these pages contain will become useful again.

The Visit 5

Sometimes owners bring the prospective horse to the center for an initial look-see, but I find it helpful to observe the horse in his or her home environment. After setting a mutually agreeable time and rounding up several member of your equine team, be sure to route the location on a map or GPS. There is nothing worse than frantically driving down a country road looking for an address that is not on a mailbox, or a barn that may or may not be visible from the road.

Be sure to allow enough time to get there. This is important because you should plan to arrive fifteen minutes early. In arriving early you sometimes find the owner in the final stages of longeing or riding the fire out of the horse. You may also witness the owner making desperate attempts to corral the hard to catch horse, or even making an attempt to cover a horse's scar or blemish with makeup or shoe polish. If you know the horse and/or owner, the early arrival probably is not necessary, but it can be quite eye-opening if you don't.

WHAT TO BRING WITH YOU

You'll want to bring a copy of the horse donation profile, and enough copies of the horse assessment form for everyone who is with you from your center. If you are high-tech, you might bring an iPad, with the forms loaded onto it, although it can be easier and more productive for your equine team members to jot down notes on the assessment form in the moment, rather than wait their turn for the iPad.

At least one person should be designated to ride the horse, so a helmet, boots, and if desired, chaps or half-chaps will come in handy. Whoever rides should be able to evaluate a horse's training, cues, and gait. The rider should be height/weight appropriate for the horse's size and build, which can be tough if you are looking at a small pony. If your center policies or procedures allow, you could bring along the young son or daughter of one of your instructors, or a small, younger sibling who can ride a pony.

This is assuming that you will use the horse for mounted activities. If there is zero chance that any staff, volunteer, or program participant will ever ride the horse, then a good ground evaluation will do, although an eye to the future is a good thing to have. Maybe, the needs of your program could change. Also keep in mind that this assessment process is one that I do for any horse, whether it is a program horse, a horse for a student, or even myself.

If the horse will also be involved (or only involved) in hippotherapy, vaulting, or driving, be sure to bring along the necessary equipment, as harness and buggy aside, the horse owner might not have those items.

WHAT TO LOOK FOR

Start with the presumption that there is no perfect horse and that no one thing will disqualify the horse from consideration. It is important to consider the horse as a whole, but you can't do that without seeing the details.

Every horse is unique. Even full brothers and sisters can look and act quite different from each other, just as they sometimes do in human families. That's why it is important to consider the horse a blank slate from the start. Your observations, and the observations of your team members, will fill in details with all of the horse's strengths and weaknesses.

After evaluating the horse from the ground (see Chapters 6-11) be sure to have the horse's owner ride or drive first. This not only allows you to see how the horse interacts with someone he knows well, it allows you to evaluate gait, movement, and willingness under saddle, which can all be quite different than when on the ground.

Plus, having the owner ride first is a good safety practice. I have seen a number of horses who have been very quiet on the ground become balky and mean tempered under saddle, even to the point of kicking, bucking, and rearing. The problem may be an ill-fitting saddle or other form of soreness, or a lack of respect for or trust in the owner. However, you don't need to observe that kind of behavior from atop the horse. Let that job fall to the owner.

It is also helpful if one person on your team can be responsible for shooting photos and/or video clips of the horse. Often, gait abnormalities or conformation faults are easier to spot in photos or on video. Plus, as you may have seen, the photo(s) provided by the owner in the horse donation profile aren't always the best.

After you have seen all you need to, tell the owner you will be in touch soon. No matter how excited you are, other team members may have concerns. Or, there may be people back at your center who could provide valuable input after looking at your assessments and watching any video you may have shot.

PART II

Conformation . . . and More 6

Entire books have been written about the conformation of the horse, and a few have been listed in the supplemental resource section (page 144). But, rather than a detailed lesson in anatomy, the conformation covered here relates to a basic assessment of the horse, along with a road map to avoid potential pitfalls and red flags.

Conformation is, essentially, the build of the horse, but there is much more that is connected, unsoundness and behavior being two of the biggest. So what, exactly, should you look for when you first see a horse? The most organized way is to start at the head and work your way back. At first this might take some time, but take all the time you need. After you've looked at several dozen horses, the process should only take a few minutes.

After you have evaluated a number of horses, you will start to see a few patterns taking place. While there are many exceptions to the rule, you will begin to see that horses with a higher neck carriage often have an up and down movement to their stride, rather than the longer, flatter movement of a horse with a lower neck carriage. You will find that horses who have a straight shoulder have a choppier trot while horses who have a big, sloping shoulder can more easily extend a gait.

It's true that conformation is more important for horses who will be ridden, driven, or vaulted on, than horses who will solely do ground work. Over time, however, poorly conformed horses have a much greater chance of developing a lameness, and accompanying stiffness or arthritis, than do horses with better conformation. This can mean high medical costs. Carrying the thought another step, a lame or stiff horse often develops bad behavior because she is uncomfortable. So, no matter what the intended purpose for the horse is, it is good to understand how well the horse might be able to do that job in five or ten years. A good evaluation of the horse's conformation is one element that will help with that understanding.

While many generalizations will be made in the following pages, think of them as something to consider, just as a doctor might consider that a child with a rash could have poison ivy. Nothing is set in stone, and all of the details are parts of the whole.

HEAD

Let's start at the top of the horse's head and work down. And, for simplicity's sake, we'll consider the ear as part of the horse's head.

EAR

The ear is the window to the horse's brain, so whatever your prospective horse's ear is pointed at is what she is thinking about. The positioning of the ear is not as important as the movement of the ear. However, some trainers feel that a horse with ears set low, toward the sides of her head, is slower to respond to a stimulus or a cue. This is not necessarily a bad thing, depending on what you want the horse to do. Ear size is often dependent on the breed. Arabians and stock horses such as the Quarter Horse, Appaloosa, and Paint can have small, dainty ears, whereas a Thoroughbred or Warmblood may have ears that are much larger.

Size aside, the ear should swivel when sound is to the horse's side or behind. A good way to test this is when the horse is relaxed, which may not be at the beginning of your evaluation. But, at the right moment, stand ten feet off the horse's hip and softly clap your hands or ring the bells you brought with you. The horse's ear should swivel toward the sound, and she may even turn her head to look for the source of the sound. You may

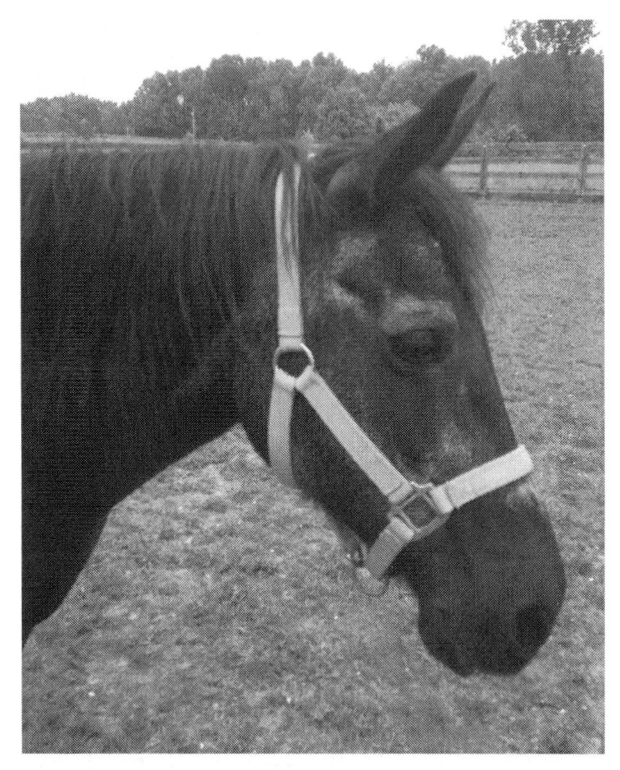

Ear size can be breed dependent. This large pony is a Tennessee Walking horse and unknown cross. Her big ears and advanced age give her face character.

want to repeat the exercise standing fifteen or so feet behind the horse. I never like to stand directly behind the horse's tail, but you can try behind the left or right hock, where the horse still has some visual of you.

If the horse gives no response, there is a chance she is hard of hearing, or even deaf. This possibility increases if the horse is older. If the horse also has a dull eye, she may have heard the sound but has shut down emotionally. Illness is another possibility. Yet another option is that the horse is so secure in her environment that she already trusts your team and you to keep her safe. Some sort of a response is a good thing because you do want the horse engaged, so you should try again in a few minutes.

EYE

Moving down to the eye, the first thing to look for are eyes that are widely-spaced. A horse whose eyes are positioned toward the side of her head, versus toward the front, can see around her much more easily. A typical horse can see almost 360 degrees around her body. There is a blind spot directly in front and directly behind, but a horse with a long, narrow face, rather than a triangular face, will have a more limited range of sight.

Horses who can't see well tend to spook. In addition, because they can't see as far around themselves as other horses can, they can be nervous. Remember that, to a horse, *everything* is about being safe. If a horse can't see that she is safe, then she will be more on edge than a horse who can. Of course, horses also use other senses to determine safety. Sight is just one of the tools a horse incorporates. But, limited range of vision limits a horse's ability to determine safety. It is something to keep in mind.

This horse has a triangular face with eyes set wide on the side of his head. His Appaloosa breeding gives him a white sclera that can be seen at the front of his otherwise soft eye.

Look, too, for a soft, kind eye. You'll know it when you see it. An eye that is dull can mean a horse is depressed, or might be sick or in pain. On the other hand, an eye that looks startled can mean the horse is jumpy. With the exception of the Appaloosa, the Pony of the Americas (POA), and a few other less common breeds, if you can see a white sclera around the eye, much like the white of a human eye, the horse might be a bit too "up." The Appaloosa, POA, and a few other breeds have been bred for many decades to show a white sclera. It is also sometimes seen in Paint horses, but if you see a lot of white around the eye in other breeds, it might be a minor red flag.

WHORL

Centuries ago, horsemen in Arabia thought the whorl pattern, or cowlick, in the center of a horse's forehead indicated how easy the horse might be to train. Gypsies in Europe, who are well known for their bond with horses, thought so too—as do many horsemen and horsewomen today.

Generally speaking, most people who have made a study of this interesting phenomenon agree that the most willing horses are those with one whorl centered on the forehead directly between the eyes. Others feel one whorl centered below the eyes is also positive.

On the other hand, the theory goes, if a horse has two (or more) swirls spread out on the face it could mean the horse has a difficult personality. I have worked with two such horses and while they were definitely a challenge, in the end they both made terrific therapy horses.

Years ago popular author and horsewoman Linda Tellington-Jones analyzed answers on a survey that was sent to horse owners. The completed surveys contained information on whorl patterns and behavior of

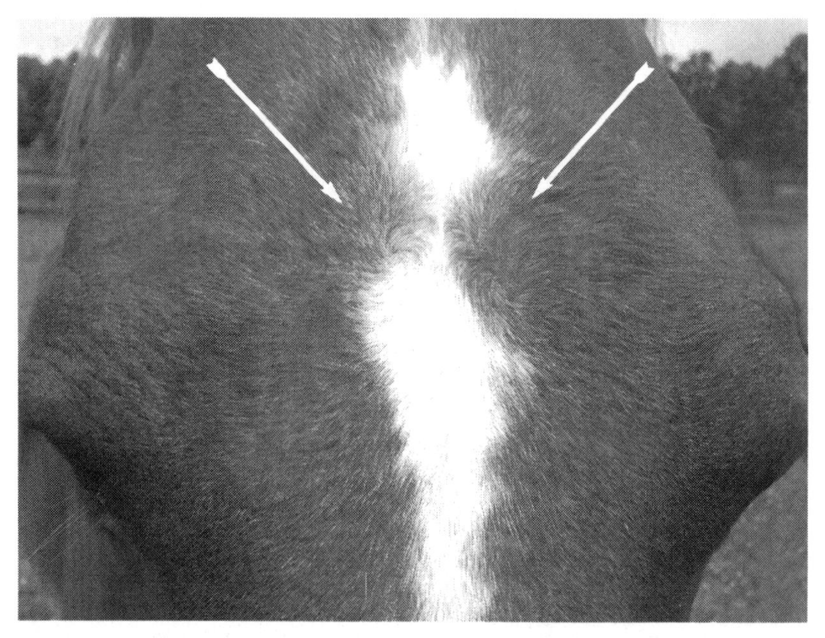

This double whorled mare is both a herd leader and a challenge. But she is also very steady and an excellent teacher.

fifteen hundred different horses and, for the most part, confirmed the following data:

- One whorl in the center of the forehead meant the horse was willing
- One whorl below the eyes indicated intelligence
- One long whorl between or running below the eyes indicated a friendly, agreeable horse
- Two or more whorls on the forehead indicated a complicated personality.

If you are fascinated by the idea that a whorl can determine personality, pick up a copy of *Getting in TTouch: Understand and Influence Your Horse's Personality* by Linda Tellington-Jones.

In addition to Tellington-Jones, English, Irish, and Polish studies all found that about 75 percent of the time left-footed horses have counterclockwise hair whorls, and horses who favor their right side have clockwise whorls. Horses with a single whorl above their eyes were more difficult, but horses who have a single whorl below or between their eyes were easier to handle. Horses with long whorls or double whorls acted the most cautiously when coming up to an unfamiliar object

The reason whorl patterns and personality are believed by many to be connected is because before a foal is born, whorl patterns and the brain form at the same time. So, should you turn down a double whorled horse? Probably not. As with everything else discussed here, it is one piece of the whole. In addition, the horse's life experiences and training can modify what nature may or may not have given him in the way of whorl patterns and behavior. Whorls are, simply, something to consider.

BRIDGE OF THE NOSE

Another conformation trait to look for is the curve of the bridge of the nose. Look at the horse from the side. Does the nose dish in, or curve out? Some of what you see is breed specific. The Arabian is one breed that dishes in, while draft horses usually curve out. The outward curve is called a Roman nose, and oddly enough, a good number of horses with Roman noses can be stubborn. Not all, by any means, but a good number of them make you work very hard for results.

NOSTRIL

Just as with humans, the nostril brings air into the lungs, and a large nostril means more air can get in. If you ride your horse on long trail rides, or if you live in higher elevations or a very hot climate, a big nostril could be very important, as your horse will have more tolerance for exercise and weather extremes.

The nostril is also used to pull in scent, so the horse can determine safety. The bigger the nostril, the more scent that can be categorized. Scent is also important in the horse's social structure within the herd. You may have noticed that most horses greet humans as they do other horses, with

This horse's large nostrils help keep her cool during hot summers in Tennessee.

their nose. Upon meeting a new horse, allowing him or her to smell the back of your hand quickly shows the horse that you are friend, rather than foe. Some people will breathe into a horse's nose, and that accomplishes pretty much the same thing.

MOUTH

The mouth of the horse you look at should be relaxed. You can see a tense mouth in the tightness of the corners of the lips, and in the lower lip. A tense mouth indicates the horse's state of mind. Some deductive reasoning may tell you why the horse is tense, but even if you never know why, it is enough to know that she is.

TEETH

A horse's teeth can tell you many things. The first indication to look for is whether or not the horse is a cribber. Cribbing is a compulsive behavior where the horse grabs a solid object, such as a stall door or fence rail with her teeth, then pulls against the object and sucks in air. Over time, cribbing can wear down the front teeth to nubs and destroy wood fences. It has also been linked as a cause of colic and stomach ulcers. Horses usually start to crib out of boredom, but once the habit starts, it is very difficult to break. You can tell if the horse is a confirmed cribber if his top front teeth are very short.

If you are unsure, at some point during the assessment casually stand the horse in front of a wood fence or panel. Keep the horse on a loose lead as you talk to the horse's owner, or amongst your equine committee. If, after five minutes or so the horse has made no move to grab the wood and suck in air, then the horse has a good chance of being okay in this area.

Windsucking is a related vice where the horse arches her neck and inhales air, without grabbing on to anything. Boredom is the root of this behavior, too, so the five-minute downtime may also root out a windsucker.

In addition to the possibilities of cribbing and windsucking, teeth can tell you the age of the horse. The sad truth is that some horse owners pass off horses as being younger than they are. Just as in our own pop culture, in the horse world, youth often rocks.

Veterinarians and seasoned horse people can often estimate the age of a horse with just a glance at his teeth. For others it is a very difficult task, especially when the horse isn't keen on showing his pearly whites. Here are two relatively easy ways to get a broad estimate of the age of a horse.

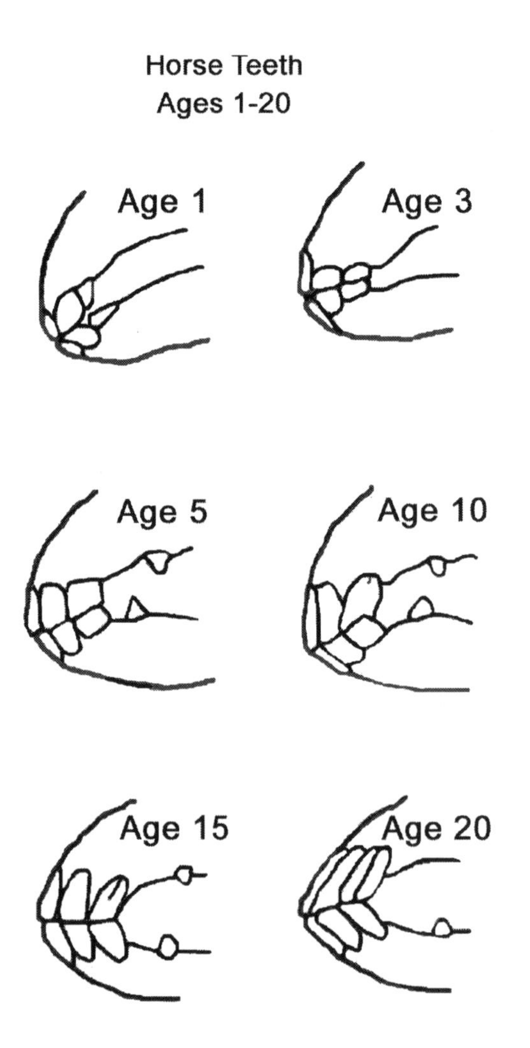

The first is a side view of the horse's front teeth. To see the teeth, part the horse's lips on the side of his mouth. Then look for the angle of the front teeth as you view them from the side. If the top and bottom teeth meet in a mostly vertical plane, then the horse is young. The greater the angle where the top and bottom teeth meet: the older the horse.

The second way to tell a horse's age, especially an older horse, is to look for Galvayne's Groove. Professor Sydney Galvayne (1846-1913) was born in the United Kingdom. A lifelong student of the horse, some considered him a horse trainer of sorts, but others saw him as a skilled self-promoter. In either case, while Galvayne did not discover the method of telling how old a horse was by looking at a groove in his teeth, he was the first to popularize it. More than a hundred years later, this interesting tooth groove still carries his name.

The groove itself occurs on the #3 upper corner incisors, and produces a vertical line beginning when the horse is ten years old. It reaches halfway down the tooth by age fifteen, and is completely down the tooth at age twenty. The groove then begins to disappear from the top of the tooth and is half gone by age twenty-five, and undetectable by age thirty. It is a simple thing to lift up the side of the horse's upper lip to see if the groove is there, and where it lies on the tooth.

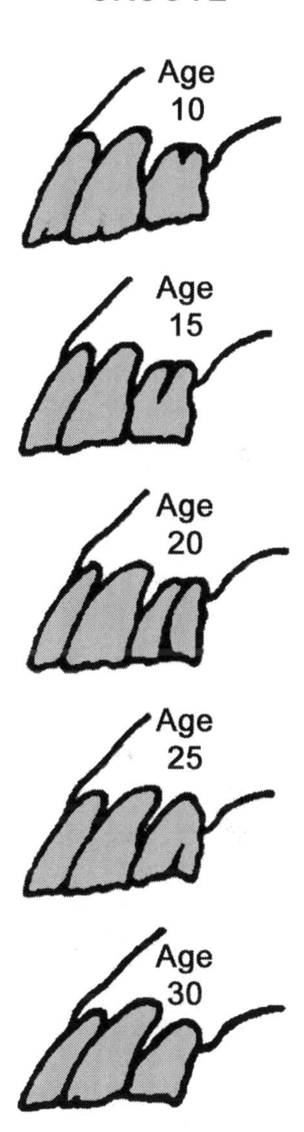

THE FRONT END

NECK

Because the horse bobs his neck up and down to propel himself forward, the size, shape, and positioning of the neck is critical to your intended use for the horse. Depending on the horse's breed, the neck of the horse you look at may be long or short, fat or thin. The important thing is that the size and shape of the neck fits the rest of the horse.

If you are looking at a breedy Thoroughbred gelding and he has a short, thick neck, it might make you think he is not fully Thoroughbred.

A short, thick neck is most often found on round, heavy horses, and these horses can eventually founder or develop Cushings syndrome.

Cushings occurs in horses when a tumor develops in the pituitary gland. As the tumor slowly grows, it sends inappropriate signals to the rest of the body to produce a lot of hormones, especially the stress hormone cortisol. Too much cortisol can be a factor in laminitis (founder), mouth ulcers, large fat deposits along the mane, excessive thirst and urination, and very long hair. Collectively, this is referred to as Cushings.

Laminitis is an inflammation within the hoof that can cause the third phalanx, a bone in the hoof that is also called the coffin bone, to rotate and cause permanent lameness. Some horses founder so badly that they cannot be saved. If the horse you are evaluating has a fat neck to match his round body, Cushings and laminitis are things to consider in the long-term management of the horse.

Generally, a horse with a long neck is more athletic than a horse with a short neck, as there is more length that the horse can use to balance himself. Also, a horse with a neck that rises upward, versus a neck that stretches horizontally in front of the body, gives the horse a more up and down movement, especially at the trot. The horse will also have more elevation of gait off the ground, and in knee and hock action. You may have ridden a horse whose springy trot made it difficult not to post too high. That horse probably had a neck that rose upward. Think Saddlebred.

This big movement at the trot is actually beneficial for many riders with autism. The more movement the horse provides, the better the rider can focus. This kind of movement also helps more independent riders get and keep their heels down. If the heels come up, the movement will throw the rider forward. It doesn't take too many times of that happening before the heels stay consistently down.

You may already have a lot of horses at your center with big movement and now need a horse who provides a smoother ride. If so, look for a horse with a horizontal neckline such as the stock type breeds usually provide. The trots are smoother, and usually there is less movement at the walk. Riders with fragile skin or those with more severe development delays can also benefit from this smoother gait.

CHEST

Next, view the width of the horse's chest from the front. Depending on the needs of your program, you may be looking for a wide horse or a narrow one. Narrow chested horses are often found in gaited breeds, such as the Tennessee Walking Horse or Spotted Saddle Horse, and in the Arabian and some Thoroughbreds.

The advantage of a narrow horse, if you do mounted work, is that riders with tight legs such as cerebral palsy, have an easier time riding as there is not too much hip and thigh stretch when they straddle the horse.

Wider chested horses can be found in the Haflinger, Fjord, draft crosses, and stock horse breeds (Quarter Horse, Appaloosa, and Paint). Many ponies also are wider, although the Hackney pony and some other breeds can be very narrow.

The advantage of width is that the wide chest provides a broad back, and riders with Down syndrome and some development delays balance

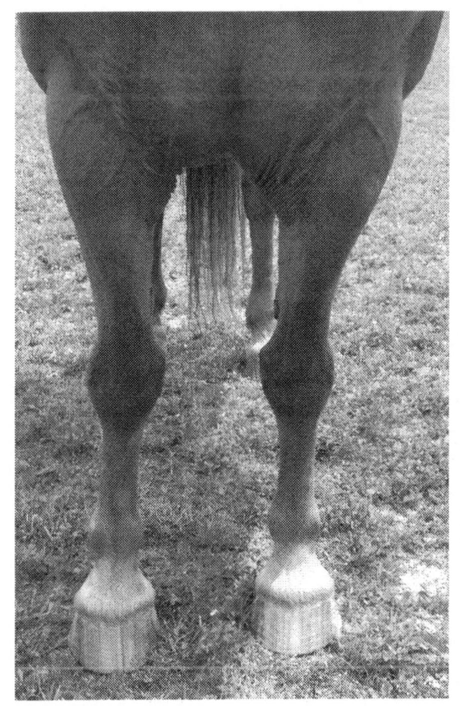

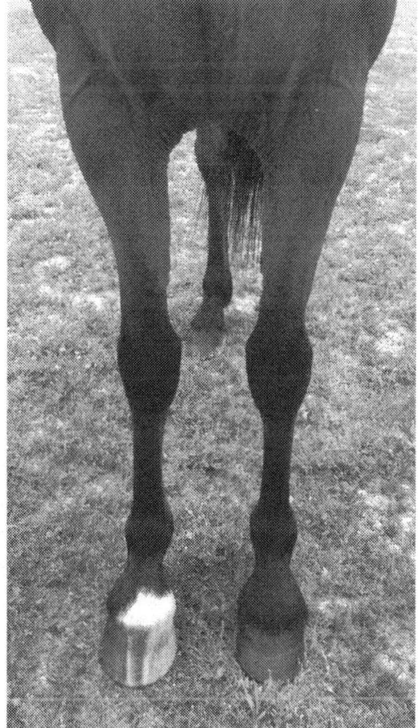

Both of these horses are 15.2, but you can easily see the very different widths of their chests and the length of their legs.

better with the wider base. Keep in mind, though, that there are variations in every rider and one individual with Down syndrome might do much better with a narrow horse. The same holds true with horses. Just because one horse is an Arabian, you can't assume that his chest will be narrow. That's another reason a thorough assessment of each horse is so important.

FRONT LEGS

The front end of the horse carries roughly two thirds of the horse's weight so it is critical that your horse's front legs be functional and sound. Finding a horse with perfect legs is impossible, but if one front hoof turns east and the other west, it is likely that your horse is bound for continual soreness and possible lameness.

Besides the fact that a horse with less than desirable front legs might be hurting (no one likes to see that), pain and soreness can cause behavior problems. When someone comes to me with a horse who behaves poorly, the first thing I do is check the horse for soreness. This is easy to do. Using light to medium pressure, run your fingers all over the horse's body, and make note of any area you touch where the horse reacts with a pinning of ears, swish of tail, or attempts at biting. We humans aren't always in the best mood when we hurt, either.

To look at the front legs, have the horse stand squarely, with all four legs evenly underneath her. Then imagine a vertical line dropping from the center of the top of the horse's front leg, all the way down to the ground. Does the line cross the center of the horse's hoof? If so, does it follow the top of the leg, through the center of the knee, and down the center of the cannon bone?

Most horses do not have faultless front leg conformation. As long as the degree to which the legs are off is not severe, there probably is no cause for worry. But, if the legs exhibit knees that point inward or outward, cannon bones that extend down from the left or right side of the knee, rather than the center, or if the horse is greatly knock-kneed or bowlegged, it could be a red flag.

The amount of bone in the cannon bone is also good to note. Bone is the thickness or heaviness of the leg. An Arabian or Paso Fino will have less bone than a draft cross. The amount of bone comes into play if there is not enough of it to support the rest of the horse. Years ago some of the stock-type horse breeders bred slim, delicate legs onto some big bodied horses. The result: much lameness and an increase in Navicular disease (or Navicular syndrome). Navicular is the inflammation of the navicular bone and surrounding tissue in the front feet and can lead to an extreme, degenerative lameness that is difficult, if not impossible, to cure. Sound horses who do not have a lot of bone typically have narrow chests and are slimmer in build.

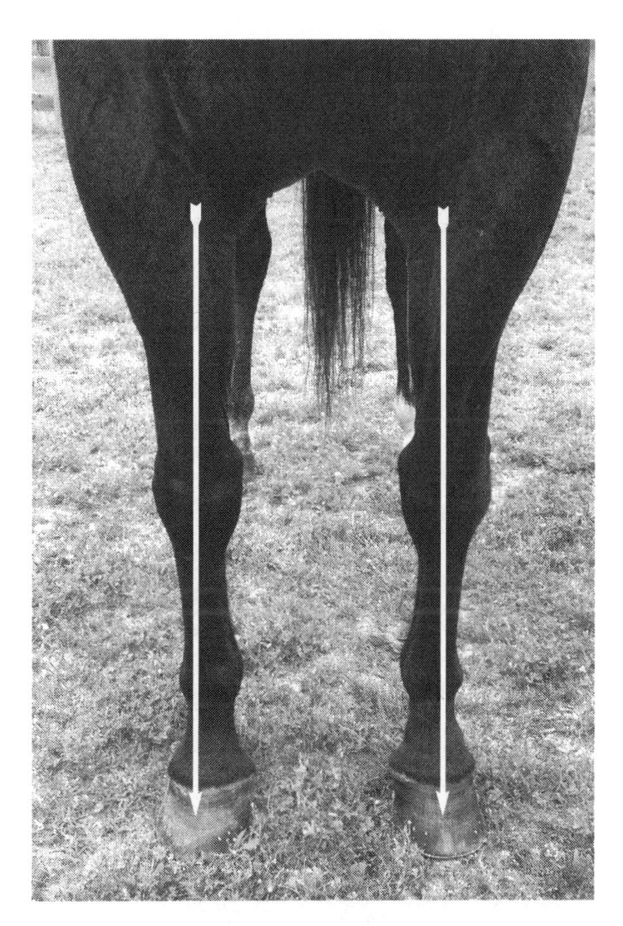

This horse is relatively straight in his upper leg, but has cannon bones and fetlocks that narrow in, and toes that point slightly out.

The amount of bone is a big factor in the amount of weight a horse can carry. Measuring a horse's cannon bone is one way to determine how much weight can be placed on a horse's back. Other methods are discussed in Chapter 7.

Cannon Bone Method:

1. With an accurate cloth tape measure, measure the circumference of the front cannon bone, just below the knee. Keep that number handy.

2. Add (A) the true weight of the horse + (B) the weight of the rider + (C) the weight of the tack.

3. Divide the total of #2 by #1 (the cannon bone circumference measurement).

4. Divide the result of #3 by two.

Hopefully you came out with a number that is between 75 and 85. If the number is greater than 85, the horse is probably not big or stout enough for your needs. While you probably can't accurately determine the horse's weight when you first look at him, an experienced member of your team can ballpark it, as long as you take a tape measure with you. In this manner, you can determine if the horse is big enough for, say, the 190 pound rider that you need the horse for.

Moving down the leg from the side, the angle of the pastern should match the angle of the horse's shoulder. The pastern and the joint nearest it, the fetlock, are shock absorbers. That's why the length of the pastern is also important. Long pasterns provide a springy ride, and short ones a choppier gait. Pasterns that are too long, however, can be weak. You will see the shorter version on draft horses, draft crosses, and some stock horses. Longer pasterns are usually seen on the Thoroughbred, Saddlebred, and many breeds of gaited horses.

SHOULDER

It is best to look at the shoulder from the side of the horse. Many who study conformation teach that the ideal shoulder is at a 45-degree angle, but across so many breeds and breed types, my experience is that the soundest horses have a shoulder angle that matches the angle of the pastern.

A straighter shoulder angle gives the horse a more up and down movement of the leg, a shorter stride, and a choppier trot. A shoulder with a greater angle will provide a longer, flatter stride and smoother trot. This is another reason that it is good to have a clear vision of the needs of your program before you look at a horse. If you have six horses with smooth trots and this is another, maybe he is not an ideal horse for you at this point in time.

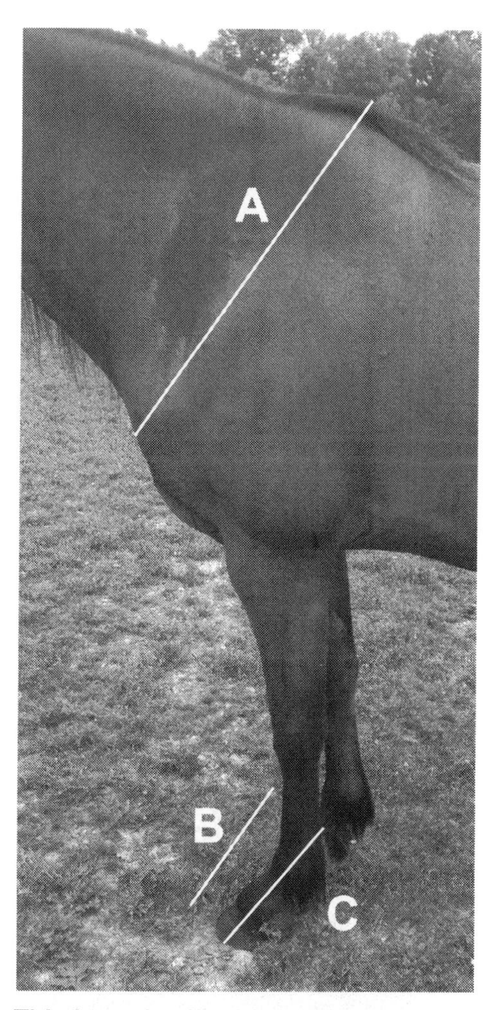

This horse's shoulder and pastern angles are nearly dead on. Lines A and B indicate the shoulder angle. Line C is the actual pastern angle.

THE MID SECTION

PROFILE

Next, stand fifteen or twenty feet away when the horse is quiet and standing square. Your first look at the horse's profile should note the height of the horse's wither as compared to the horse's hip. Which is higher? Note that a horse with a wither that is higher will also often have a more vertical neck, and higher action from the front legs. This is referred to as "uphill."

If the hip is higher, the horse is considered "downhill." The neck of a downhill horse will most often be more level with the wither and the stride flatter, more horizontal. The first type of conformation produces a lot of choppy movement at the trot, the second a lot of movement at the walk. Knowing the needs of your program participants is helpful. Will the horse, for example, serve more able-bodied riders with autism, or riders with developmental delays who won't do a lot of trotting, but who can benefit from the big movement at the walk? More on gait and movement will be discussed in Chapter 12, but it is good to think of those things as you get your first full glimpse of the horse.

This pony's topline is clearly higher at the hip than at the withers, which gives her riders a lot of pelvic movement.

The second and more important consideration in your assessment of the horse's profile is the shape of the horse's middle section. In your mind's eye, draw a line across the top of the wither to the top of the croup and extend to above chest and the point of the buttocks. Then drop the line vertically to the ground, and across the ground until it joins with a line dropped from the chest. This gives a four-sided shape and this shape is important to the movement of the horse.

You will see one of three shapes: a square, a rectangle, or a tall rectangle. Some shapes are breed dependent. A Saddlebred, Morgan, Rocky Mountain Horse, and some sport horse type Warmbloods tend to be tall rectangles. (The vertical distance from ground to wither and ground to the high point of the croup is greater than the horizontal distance between point of shoulder and point of buttock.) These horses have very long legs! There are exceptions, but to go with the tall rectangle, you often find vertical necks, tail set high on the croup, and front end elevation in the gait.

Turn the tall rectangle sideways to get a horse who is longer on the topline than from ground to wither or ground to top of croup. Many stock-type breeds have this kind of profile, and the lower neck carriage

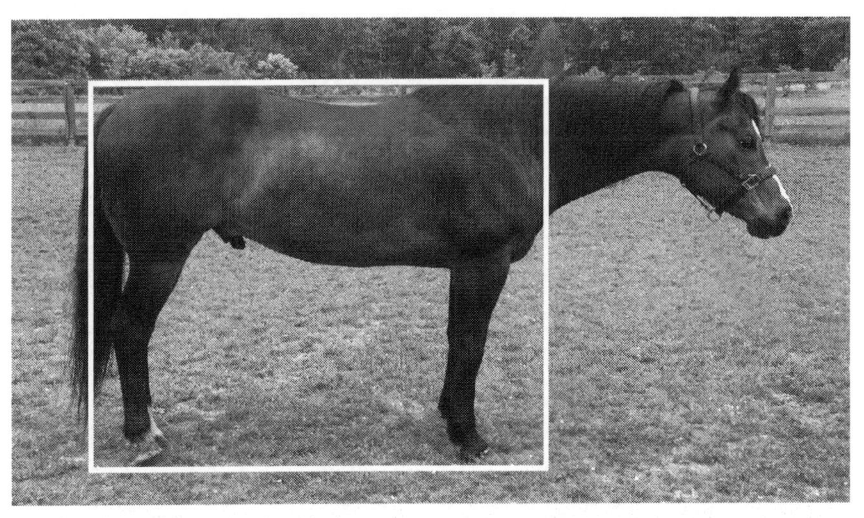

The dimensions of the white line above are 2.5 inches across and 2.06 inches down, indicating this gelding has a long topline and a rectangular shape.

and tail set to go with it. None are either good or bad, with the exception of a very long rectangle, which means the horse has an unusually long back. This long back can be the source of soreness, and many horses with long backs need a lighter rider weight limit, as compared to a horse with a shorter back.

If the horse will only be part of ground lessons, a very long back is still of importance to you because of the potential for soreness. Many horses who are never ridden (or have not been ridden in a long time) are sore, and that can turn into a behavioral issue, or a series of expensive and ongoing veterinary calls, massages, acupuncture treatments, and the like. It is important not to generalize, as not all horses with long backs are sore, but to take note of likelihoods and then put all the information together before you make a decision.

Sometimes it is easier to see in a photo which profile shape a horse has, and this should be a shot that one of your team members takes. This is especially true if you plan to take the horse's information back to staff at the center, or to an able-bodied rider or her parents if the horse is being considered for an individual.

WITHER

The wither is, of course, the bony protrusion at the front of the horse's back, and it also ties into the neck. Some horses have very tall withers, and some have hardly any withers at all. I have even seen both extremes within the same breed, and both extremes present their own set of difficulties.

The high withered horse can be difficult to saddle fit. Here, the withers are too high to give adequate clearance for the front of the saddle. Also, the front of the saddle on a high withered horse often tips the seat of the saddle backward, causing the rider to ride out of balance with the horse. Saddles that do not fit the horse are probably the number one cause of soreness in horses. As mentioned earlier, soreness can cause behavior problems and, if left untreated, possible lameness. Think of a professional athlete who has a sore back. Eventually he (or she) will begin to walk differently to accommodate the soreness, and that difference in gait can put further wear and tear on other areas of the shoulders, back, hips and legs. Twenty years down the road, horse or human, the old pro has a permanent gimp in his gait.

The low withered horse can also be difficult to fit to a saddle, because there is no wither to help hold the saddle in place. Those horses often have saddles that slip from side to side, which is a huge safety hazard. A low withered horse can also become sore because it is difficult to center the saddle evenly on the horse's back. To counter act that, many people cinch or girth the horse too tightly in an attempt to keep the saddle from slipping, and that can cause pain.

The last thing to look for in the wither is that it is evenly developed on both the left and right sides. I have looked at several horses who had past injuries to the wither area. One had somehow fallen on his back after jumping over the pasture fence and fractured several bones in his withers. In addition to having uneven withers left and right, he walked with his shoulders hunched. He was a lovely, agreeable fellow, but probably would not have held up for a lot of riding, or riding by heavy riders. I was glad to hear he found a wonderful home at a program that allowed his great personality to shine. His new job was to help senior humans stay active and he was groomed everyday and taken for walks by people who were in their eighties.

Horses who perform the same job over a long period of time can also build muscle differently on the left and right sides of their withers. Polo and barrel racing are two sports that come to mind, as they require a horse to bend more in one direction than the other.

POSTURE

As with the horse with the broken withers, the posture of the horse is very important. Posture is different from conformation in that it is how the horse stands, versus how the horse is built. Does the horse have a dull eye, or is the tail clamped? Are the shoulders hunched? Legs too far underneath her? Does she walk with a stride that is shorter than what you would expect?

Those are all signs of pain, and the horse's posture reflects that. I have a Jack Russell/Chihuahua mix, Abby, who was born with shallow kneecaps. When she was young her knees dislocated a few times, and while there technically is surgery to correct that, for many reasons her veterinarian felt Abby was not a good candidate. Over time, Abby has developed an odd, wide stance behind and while at age eight she still can chase a squirrel with the very best, it is hard for her to raise her head and neck as high as she used to. She sometimes stands with her back bowed up, and when this happens I know she needs a puppy massage before her next session with the squirrels.

Poor posture can be difficult to see in some horses, but it is best seen in profile. Posture will further come into play in Chapter 8 when the horse's range of motion is factored in.

BARREL

The barrel of the horse covers the horse's sides, and there are two kinds: flat and round. Flat barrels are more often seen on high withered, high necked, tall rectangle horses, while rounder barrels are seen on the lower, longer horses.

It is important not to mistake fat, or lack of it, for the shape of the barrel, and sometimes feeling the horse's sides is the best way to assess. The shape of the barrel is important for several reasons. First, inside the barrel is where the horse stores all of his internal organs, including his lungs. While therapy horses rarely need huge lung power, such as that to win a race or compete in an endurance ride, the lung capacity of a horse does come into play in extreme hot or cold temperatures, or at high altitudes. The more air a horse can pump in, the more easily the horse can tolerate extremes.

For those horses who will be ridden, the width the barrel provides is important. If you need the horse for riders with CP, then a flatter barrel will keep the rider from having too much stretch in his or her leg. If a rider needs the stability of a broader back, however, you can usually find that on a horse with a wider barrel.

Most critical, though, is that the horse's left and right barrel are mostly even. To look, stand ten to fifteen in front of the horse and look at the shape of the barrel. Is the roundness even on both sides? For riders who need an even, symmetrical horse and movement, this evenness in the shape of the barrel is critical.

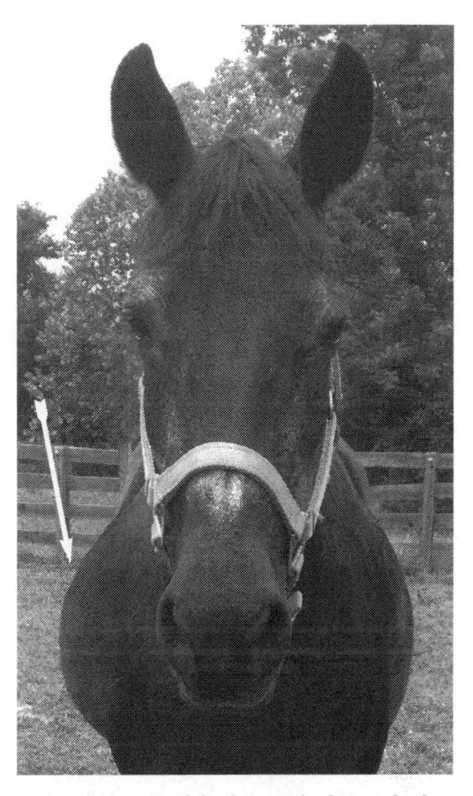

In looking at this horse's barrel, the cecal swing on the right side is apparent.

One reason both sides of the horse's barrel might not be similar is due to arthritis and/or muscle atrophy. If the horse is older, but once worked hard at polo, cutting, barrel racing, or another such sport, this might be the case. A few rubs or pats on both sides will allow you to check the area for soreness.

You might see that the right side of the horse is larger than the left. The horse stores much of her food in the cecum, which is on the right side of her body. When the horse has eaten a lot of forage, the right side of her barrel may bulge outward and when she walks toward you, you will see a large left and right swing of her belly. This is called the cecal swing. Depending on what the horse ate, or didn't eat, before you arrived, you may not see much of a swing. Some horses have a huge cecal swing, while others, even with a belly full of hay, do not have much at all.

Regardless of the cause, an uneven barrel can put unbalanced riders even more off-balance. If the rider's left leg drops vertically on a flat barreled horse, but the rider's right leg has to spread outward at the hip to accommodate a large cecal swing or more muscle development on the right

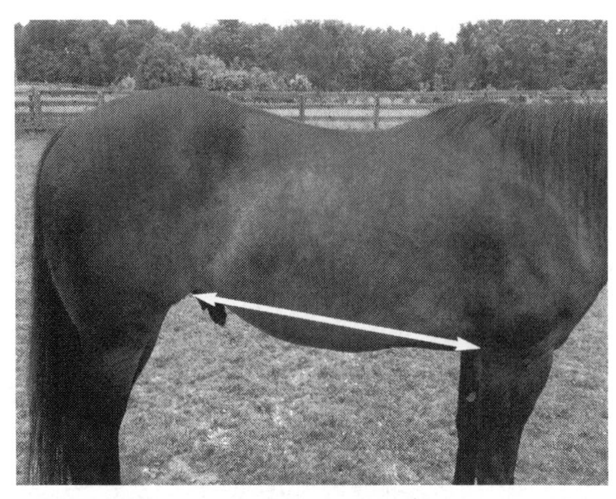

While not in top physical condition, the belly line on this gelding shows him to be relatively fit and of appropriate weight.

side, this horse might not be a suitable mount for some riders.

STOMACH

The horse's stomach is best viewed from the side. Ideally, you will see a straight line from the horse's elbow to where the underside ties into the gaskin. That's a sign of a healthy, fit horse. If the belly dips downward, the horse you are looking at might be out of shape, or too fat. Sometimes it's hard to see past a big hay belly, which will go away with diet and exercise.

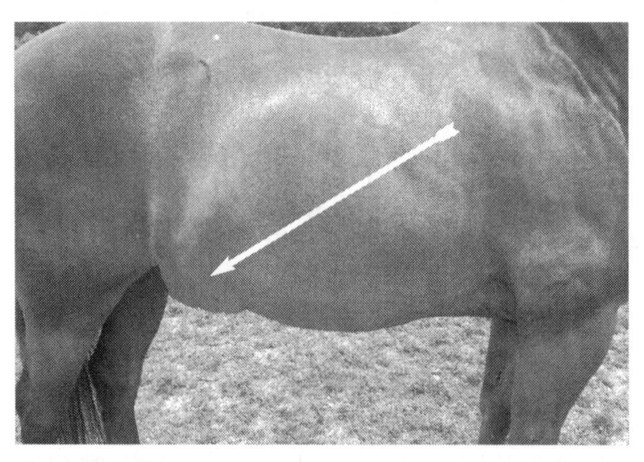

Horses of all breeds and ages can get a hernia. Some will limit a horse's activity, some not.

Worms can also cause a hay belly, and a look around the horse's living space to see if manure is left to pile up will give an indication if this is a cause. This is another good reason to have the horse's vet records in hand before you visit. In years past, veterinarians did a lot of the worming, but today, with improvements in medications and products, most equine caregivers take care of the worming themselves. You might, however, see on the vet record if the veterinarian has wormed the horse, or made note of the product the owner used, and when.

A final cause of a low underline might look like a hay belly, but be a hernia. Horses of all breeds and ages can get a hernia and there are many causes. Often, but not always, the hernia is seen toward the back of the belly as an uneven bulge. Most hernias are of minor concern for EAAT.

BACK

We will talk about the horse's loin and croup in the next sections, but as a general rule of thumb, the horse's back, loin, and croup (the distance from the back of the wither to the top of the tail) should be about equal in length. Horses with long backs and short loins are seen more often than the other way around and the problem with that is a long back can be a weak back. If the horse is to be ridden, and this includes vaulting, a weak back means the horse can carry less weight than a shorter backed horse

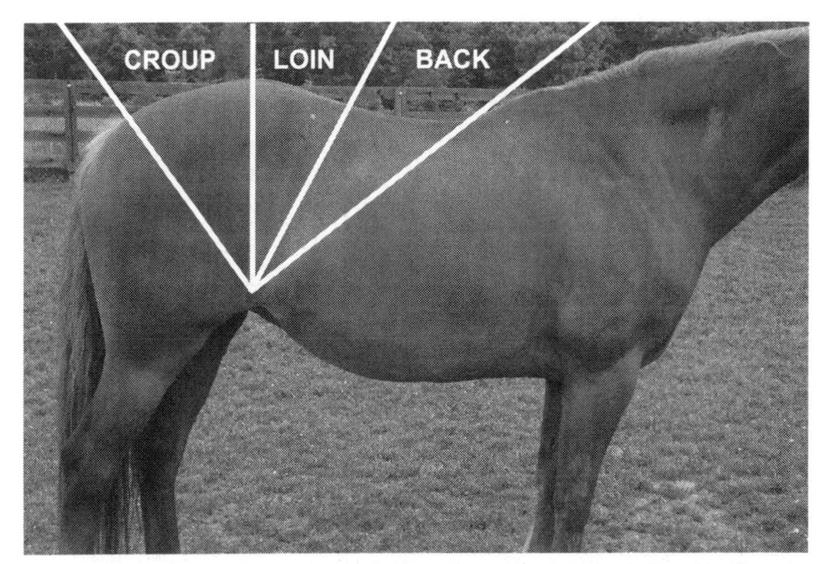

This horse is a little long in the croup, as compared to the back and loin. The length of the croup is important because it is the "engine" that powers the horse. A long croup also houses more muscle mass. Many horses are long in the back or loin and short in the croup, which weakens the horse's rear power pack.

of the same size, age, breed, bone, and condition. A long back also makes it harder for the horse to round out her back to engage her hindquarters for collection. And, the back is more prone to muscle strain, especially as the horse ages.

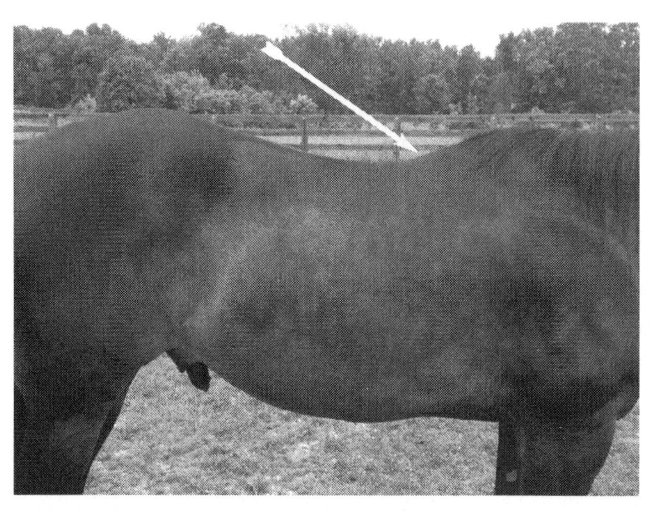

At fifteen, this horse's back has dropped over the past few years. By age twenty, it will most likely have dropped even more.

On the very big plus side, a longer back can be more flexible, and the movement provided by this kind of back can provide a smooth ride.

In addition to the length of the back, also note how level it is. An older, long backed horse might be sway backed. When the center of the back drops, it becomes difficult to find a saddle that fits. What usually happens then is that the weight of the saddle and rider bridges, or opens up a gap in, the low center of the horse's back and only puts weight where the front and back of the saddle touch the horse. This causes soreness and can result in behavior problems. No one, horse or human, likes to work when they hurt.

Finally, look for adequate padding over the entire backbone. If the backbone is raised, it could be the horse is thin, and needs to gain weight. Or, you could again be looking at muscle atrophy. That important layer of padding along the spine is not all fat. Instead, it is muscle that helps the horse move forward and support the rider, so it is important that there be enough of it. That muscle helps the horse "use" her back effectively. Some horses, however, such as big, rangy, older Thoroughbreds, always seem to have a protruding backbone and are just fine for many purposes. It is just one other area for you to consider.

LOIN

The loin is the area between the horse's lower ribs and pelvis and is where the lumbar vertebrae are located. As with the back, it should be roughly one third of the distance from the wither to the top of the tail. Most horses have six lumbar vertebrae, but some breeds, such as the Arabian, have five. Regardless of the number, they are the largest of the horse's vertebrae.

The loin connects the horse's hindquarters and front end. This is where power from the hindquarters transfers to the front when the horse moves. The loin should be short, strong, and muscled, so a concern would be if the horse is sore in this area. If the loin is weak or sore, the horse will have a difficult, painful time supporting the weight of a rider.

For unmounted work, keep in mind that a horse with soreness or stiffness in the back and loin can still be an excellent teacher, especially if

It is interesting to see that the horse does not have a back "bone," but instead has many spiky vertical "fingers" of bone.

the soreness is temporary. This horse may require extra in the way of vet care and supplements, but if you are prepared to do that and the horse checks out in many other areas, it might be worth it to give her a try.

THE BACK END

CROUP

Depending on the breed of your horse, the croup may be flat or sloped. Arabians, Standardbreds, Walking Horses and other breeds with a narrow build and high neck carriage also have a flatter croup. This area is the final of the "thirds," and should be about equal in length to the back and loin.

The croup should be uniform in width, muscular, and even across the top. The length of the croup is associated with speed and endurance, while the width is associated with strength or power. Horses with flatter croups are often good jumpers, as they have a long stride and can get their hind legs way out behind them. Those with more slope to the croup, such as the Quarter Horse, can get their hind legs underneath and push off with great power in many short strides. But, a croup that is too steep can indicate weak hip and hocks.

HIP

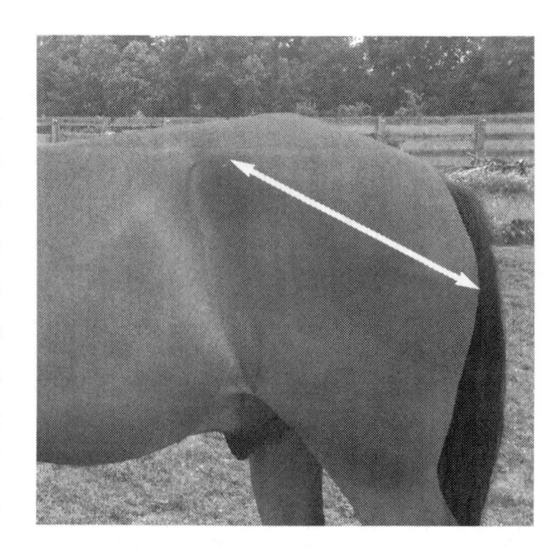

The hip refers to a line running from the ilium (the point of the hip) to the ischium (the point of the buttock). The key point to look for here is that the hips are even. To determine this, stand well behind the horse. Be sure all four of the horse's feet are placed squarely underneath him, then find the point of the left and right hip.

On a heavy horse this may be harder to see, but your equine committee can help. Have one person stand on each side of the horse, and place his or her index finger on the point of the horse's hip. Each point of hip should be an equal distance from the ground. If one hip is higher than the other, think arthritis, injury, or even a decreased range of motion on one side, which will cause an uneven gait.

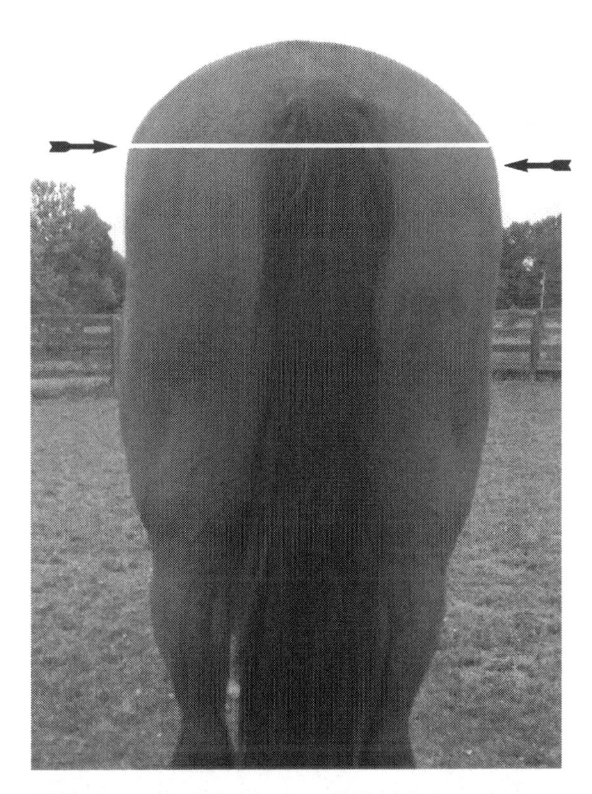

This horse's left hip is a little higher than his right.

Uneven hips provide uneven movement for the rider. The trot or gaited movement will be dissimilar behind, and the horse may lope or canter without one or both back legs reaching underneath his belly. If an even, continuous, symmetrical gait is important to you,

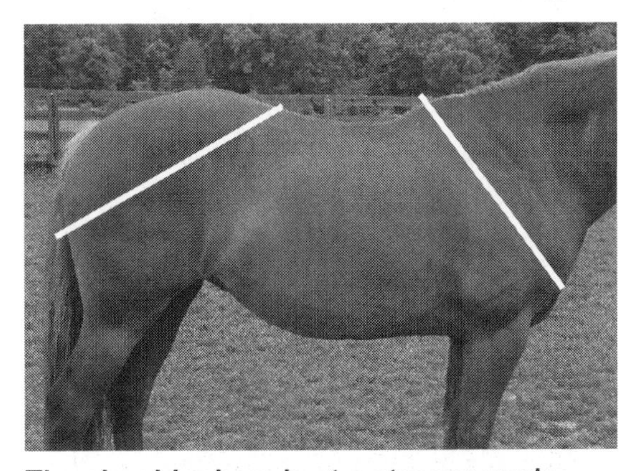

The shoulder here is at a steeper angle than the hip. This mare has a choppy trot, but provides a lot of rider pelvic movement at the walk.

this horse will not be able to provide it at this point in time. Only a veterinarian or equine chiropractor can tell you the extent of the situation—or if it can be remedied.

Then, from the side, look at the angle of the hip and the angle of the shoulder. The two angles should be a reverse match of each other. Horses who have matching angles seem to be more athletic, have a better chance at staying sound, and have the ability to collect easily.

BACK LEGS

While the front legs bear most of the weight of the horse, it's the back legs that provide the power for the horse to move forward. Before looking at your prospective horse's back legs, it is important to understand some of the structure of the leg. The horse's back leg starts at the stifle, which is the joint nearest the line of the belly, and is also the largest single joint in the horse's body. It is the equivalent of the human knee, and like the knee, helps the horse's hind leg stay firmly planted on the ground.

Moving down the leg, the next joint is the hock, which is similar to the human ankle, and the point of the hock, the human heel. The rear pastern is, like the front, a shock absorber, but because most of the horse's weight is borne on the front legs, the angle of the rear pastern should be a little steeper than in the front, which adds strength to the joint.

From the side, your horse's hocks should be clean, with no swelling or scar tissue. A capped hock, or bursitis of the hock, is the result of an injury and is noticed by a swelling on the point of the hock. This swelling may or may not be permanent, and there may or may not be lameness associated with it. A capped hock is relatively common as injuries go, and something to both look for and consider.

The hock also helps propel the horse forward, and sports that put a lot of twist on the hock, such as cutting, polo, and reining, can over time cause arthritis, or weakness in this joint. As with the front legs, when standing behind the horse, you should be able to drop a vertical line from the top of the leg, through the center of the hock and cannon bone, down through the back of the hoof.

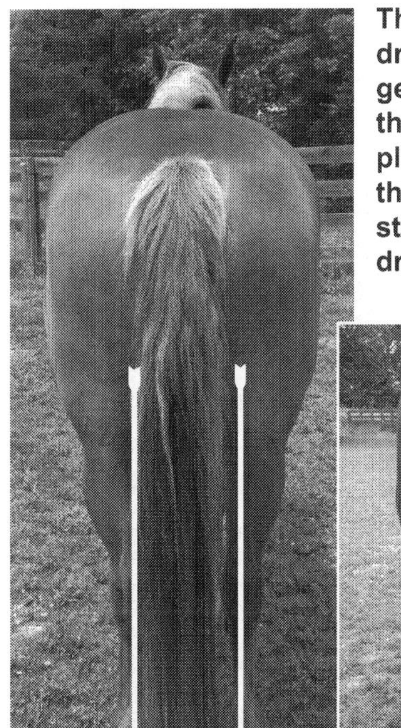

This Belgian cross (left), like many draft horses, is cow hocked. For generations, draft horses were bred that way so they could step in the ploughed furrows without breaking the lines. The horse below is structurally better, with the line dropping straight through the hock, cannon bone, and the back of the hoof.

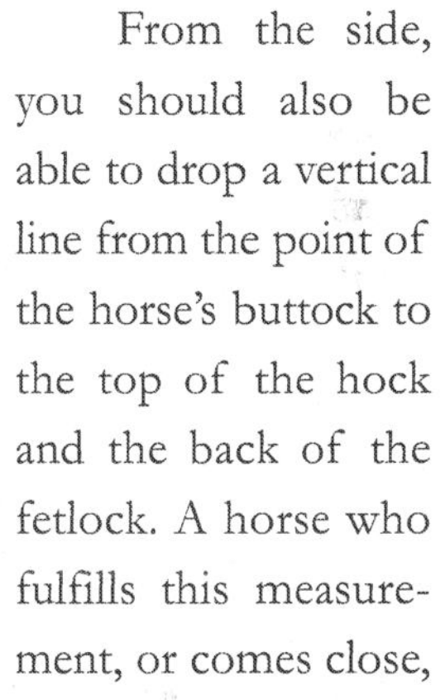

From the side, you should also be able to drop a vertical line from the point of the horse's buttock to the top of the hock and the back of the fetlock. A horse who fulfills this measurement, or comes close, can carry weight well and also reach under him- or herself to propel forward.

In looking at your prospective horse, keep in mind what you need the horse to do. Every horse will have some deviation from these guidelines, but extreme deviation may mean an unsoundness or extra expense to keep the horse comfortable.

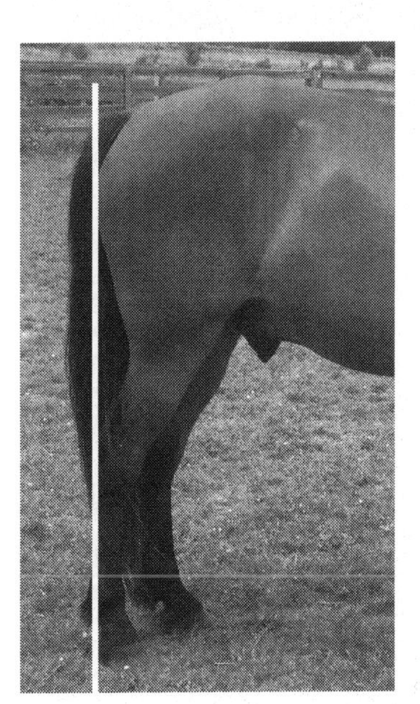

This Walking Horse reaches well under himself and overtracks well.

TAIL

The horse's tail serves many purposes. In addition to being an excellent fly swatter, it is a communication tool, windbreak, protection device, and helps balance the horse. If you are in a cold or windy climate, a long, thick tail keeps wind and cold from racing between the horse's back legs and to the underside of the horse's body, where hair often is not as thick. Ever hear the old adage about a horse turning his tail to the wind? That's why.

A tail held to one side may indicate pain.

The tail is also part of the horse's spinal column and can be a good indicator of soundness or soreness. First, stand behind the horse when he is standing square on all four feet. Is the tail carried loosely and evenly between the horse's butt cheeks? Or, is the top of the tail cocked to one side?

Next watch the horse's tail as he walks straight away from you. Is the tail still loose and even, or is it held to one side? If the horse carries his tail to the left or right, there may be soreness or arthritis over the lumbar vertebrae, hips, or even farther up the back. You won't know how severe the issue is until you get an equine medical professional in to evaluate, but the problem should be noted.

Often, a cocked tail is just minor soreness and can be worked out with massage, acupuncture, or chiropractic adjustments. If the cocked tail has been left untreated for many months or years, however, then arthritis may have developed, which will be much harder to manage.

The tail is a very important tool when it comes to balance. The horse will move his tail left or right to round corners or counter act the weight of an unbalanced rider, so if the horse has limited movement in his tail, trotting balanced around a corner or carrying an unwieldy rider could be very difficult. As you assess this horse, keep an eye on his tail, as he will communicate to you with it. Every swish, clamp, or up and down flap means something, even if he is just telling a fly to get lost.

IN GENERAL

HOOVES

Not everyone wants the expense of taking care of their horse's hooves properly, especially when they want to find the horse another home. Hopefully the horse you are looking at has had a recent trim or shoe reset, but do not be surprised if she hasn't.

Long, untrimmed feet can make the horse stand awkwardly and it can be hard to get an accurate assessment of the horse's conformation if this is the case. Long toes can throw off shoulder and pastern angles, posture, and gait, and even cause soreness. Sometimes you have to use a "best guess" or even your imagination.

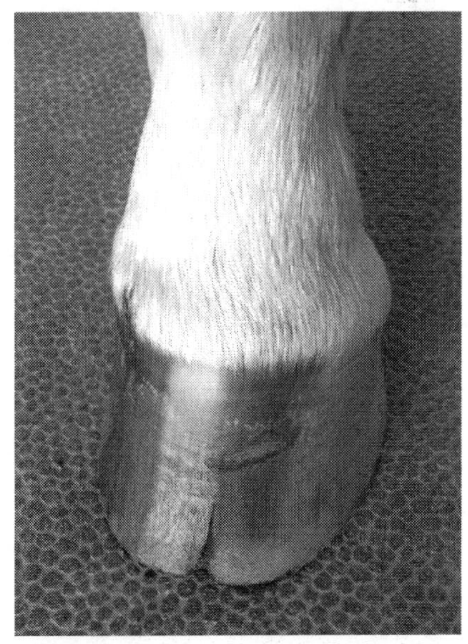

A vertical split may or may not cause lameness. A crack such as this may also cause the horse to compensate on other limbs and become sore across his hips, shoulders, and back.

Specifics to look for within the hoof include vertical cracks, as these can be difficult and expensive to make go away. The hardness and thickness of the hoof wall is also important. Some horses are prone to "shelly" or crumbly hooves. These hooves break down easily if the horse is barefoot or if the hoof wall is too thin to hold a shoe nail. Nutrition and environmental factors, such as an extremely dry climate play a part in the shelly hoof, but so do genetics, injury, and lack of proper trimming.

Some draft or heavy horses are prone to a flare of the hoof, especially near the heel. A flare is actually a separation of the hoof wall from the coffin bone. Flares can be caused by many things and can happen to any horse. Usually the condition

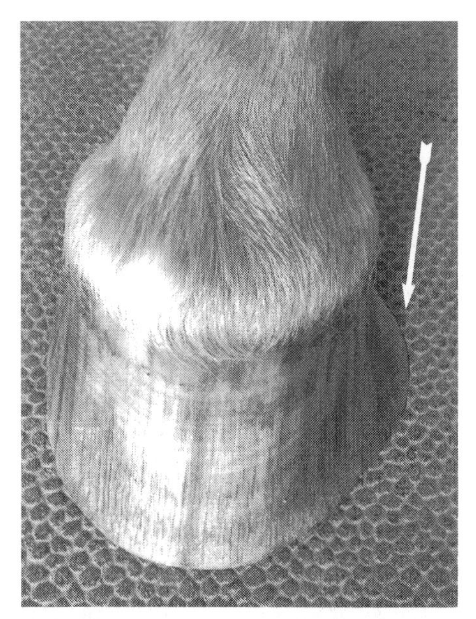

This kind of flare is often seen on draft horses and on draft crosses.

can be corrected, and often it is not serious, but if left untreated, it can become painful. Genetics, founder, lack of trimming, and an extremely wet climate can all contribute, but you may have to use your detecting skills to find out both the cause and the solution.

A quick note on hoof color. Hoof color can range from light tan to black, to every shade between. Some horses even have vertical stripes on their hooves. As a rule, a horse with a white stocking that goes down to the hoof wall will have a white hoof. A horse with a dark lower leg will have a dark hoof. The exception is a white horse who may technically be a gray. Many gray horses are born black and then "gray" out. Those horses have dark skin and hooves, unless he or she has a white stocking.

This Walking horse's dark leg shows a striped hoof.

Some people feel that white hooves are softer than dark. An old cowboy saying is: *Four white feet and a white nose, cut off his head and throw him to the crows.* Of course, we don't want to do that! But back in the 1800s on a ranch when there was little in the way of hoof care (or sunburn care for noses) one can see that a horse with hard, dark hooves and a dark nose might be preferable to the cowboy who was out on the range for weeks at a time. Many farriers and trimmers, however, will tell you that a light hoof is just as good as a darker one.

A few breeds, such as the Appaloosa and Pony of the Americas, have vertical stripes on the hoof wall. Because Appaloosa, Quarter Horse, and Paint horses have some of the same foundation sires, you can sometimes see striped hooves in the latter two breeds and even with select horses in just about any breed.

The bottom line is whether or not the hoof is healthy enough for the horse's intended purpose. Will the hoof hold up for the activities the horse will be doing? And, how much will it cost to maintain that healthy hoof? Unfortunately, at most centers budget is a consideration. Your program just might not have the funds to care for a horse who will incur higher than average veterinarian or shoeing bills.

MUSCLE TONE

The tone and amount of muscle on the horse you have gone to look at is important, too. Some stock-type horses and draft or draft crosses have a large amount of heavy, bulky muscle. These are often strong horses with wide backs. Arabians, the Hackney Pony and other such breeds are lighter muscled and can, as a whole, move very quickly.

Whichever kind of muscle the horse has, it is important that it be evenly distributed on both the left and right sides of the horse. It seems as though it would be, but there are many instances where that is not the case.

Older horses who have been mounted from the ground all their lives often have different muscling on the left and right sides of their shoulders, back, and barrel. This is because the horse has to brace for the twisting motion of the saddle that accompanies the mount. Over time, the horse builds asymmetrical musculature. This can make it difficult to find a saddle to fit the different sides of the horse, and can cause misalignment in the bones of the back, as well as arthritis.

In addition, horses who are involved in activities that require the horse to perform the same moves over and over can also develop differently from left side to right. Polo ponies are a good example. In polo, the rider usually swings the mallet from the right side of the horse. As a protective measure the horse begins to move with his head, neck, and hips canted to the left. This is to reduce the chance that the horse might mistakenly be hit with the mallet. Over time, the horse begins to move with a decided curve to the left and builds up different muscle tone on the left and right sides of his body. From experience, it is a time consuming process to get a seasoned polo pony to walk straight. Some, due to arthritis and atrophy, will always be dissimilar left and right in both their movement and their muscle tone.

That said, polo ponies typically make great therapy horses. They have experienced so much that they are generally unflappable, get along well in the herd, and are willing and easy-going. Physical issues aside, I look very closely are any polo horse offered as a therapy horse, for there is a lot of good there.

Two other sports that can make a horse develop differently are barrel racing (more left turns than right) and roping (some of the same left cant to the head and neck as with the polo horses).

SCARS AND BLEMISHES

Scars and blemishes may be unsightly, but they are not necessarily harmful to the horse's soundness or well-being. The difference between the two is simple. A scar is the leftover of an accident to the skin or underlying soft tissue and may or may not be deep or involve surrounding areas. A blemish is the result of an injury, poor conformation, or overuse that results in lumps, large or small, usually near joints or on the long bones of the legs.

In looking at scars, the location often determines if there will be any serious effect on the horse. First, look for a big, noticeable scar. The current owner may be able to tell you about it, how it got there, and how long ago. Then run your hands over the horse's body to find smaller scars and blemishes, such as warts or other lumps. Some of these can be covered by the horse's hair, especially in colder months. The running of your hands also accomplishes another purpose, that of checking the horse for soreness.

If you find a scar on a joint, or in a location that would be covered by a girth, saddle, or bridle, pay special attention. I once worked with a horse who developed a large wart under his belly near his front legs, right where the girth went. He was fine at some times, and cranky at others. We finally realized the wart was there and, depending on which girth was used, he sometimes was uncomfortable when saddled. The wart was easily removed, though, and once he healed he was fine. Scars over a joint, if severe enough, can cause intermittent or even permanent unsoundness.

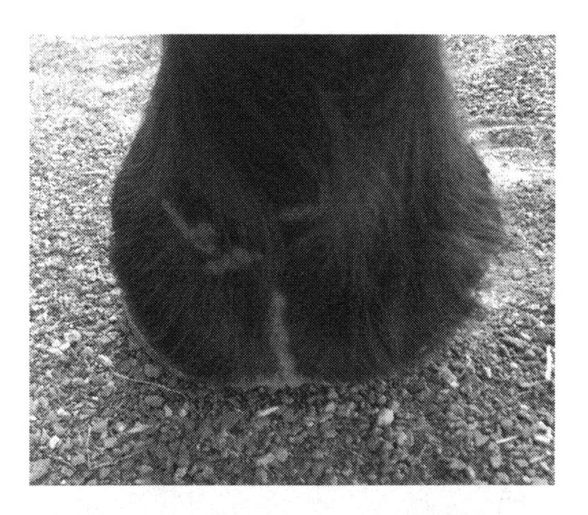

Even though these scars are old, the original injury was enough to make this front hoof different in size and shape from the other front hoof. This horse is often gimpy when barefoot, but does fine with a set of front shoes.

A blemish, in turn, can be a fluid filled lump, such as a wind puff (usually caused by poor conformation, injury, or overuse), capped elbow (often caused by a horse knocking the elbow with a front shoe when lying down), or a harder lump, such as a splint (a bony deposit on the upper inside of the front cannon bone). Or, a blemish can initially be an unsoundness or lameness, such as a bowed tendon that when healed, causes no problem. Blemishes usually do not interfere with riding, although they are frowned upon in the show ring, especially in conformation or halter classes.

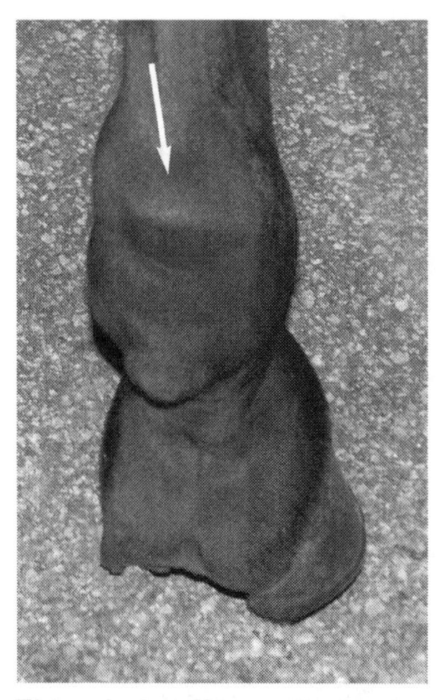

This wind puff is on the back of the fetlock, but causes the horse no pain or loss of range of motion.

As a whole, all of this can seem like a great deal to look for, but with a little practice, you can learn to assess all of the attributes for an individual horse in less than five minutes. You will develop the skill of looking at the side view of the horse and taking it all in at once: the angles of the shoulder and pasterns, levelness of wither and hips, height of the neck set, tightness of the belly, look of the eye, and more.

As you move through the assessment, you can add this information to the information you already have: age, training, size, etcetera, along with information we have yet to cover, such as gait and flexibility. Soon, you will have a full picture of the horse and can make a decision as to whether or not he or she will be a valued addition to your herd.

Size and Build 7

The size and build of the horse matters a great deal and are dependent on the needs of your program. If you have many young children who have just begun with your center, you should look to your needs now—and for several years in the future. How old are the kids? What is the ratio of boys to girls? This is important, because when many of the boys hit puberty and develop into young men, they will require much larger horses. Not all of your twelve-year-old program riders will grow into six-foot-two, two hundred pound sixteen-year-olds, but some will.

What disabilities does your center serve? If you have a number of riders with CP, you will need a higher number of narrow horses than a center that only provides therapeutic driving. Does your center have a large group of vaulters? Then you will most likely need several wide horses.

In looking at your prospective horse, be sure to keep the needs of your program in mind. It is hard to turn away the "perfect" 14 hand narrow pony, but if you already have six similar ponies, then maybe one of the existing small horses should be retired before a new one officially joins the herd.

It seems that most centers continually looks for the elusive big, versatile horse, one that is 16 hands, not too wide, not too old, is gentle without having too big a stride; and can walk, trot, and canter with a slightly unbalanced rider who weighs 180 pounds. Those horses are worth their weight in gold. If you see one that you can't incorporate into your program, a referral to a nearby center will most likely be appreciated. That goes for any horse who looks promising, but for reasons of size, build, or other circumstance will not fit your needs.

If the amount of weight the horse can carry is of concern to you (and if your participants ride, it should be), know that the maximum weight a horse can carry varies by breed, age, size, conditioning, conformation, and the level of the work she will be expected to do. Generally speaking, a light-framed 15 hand horse can carry less weight than a stoutly built horse of the same size. One way to determine how much weight the horse can carry was given in Chapter 6. Here are two others:

20 PERCENT RULE

In this method, a 1,000-pound horse can carry 20 percent of her weight, or 200 pounds of rider and tack. The key is in knowing exactly how much your horse weighs, which can be difficult if you do not have a scale for your horse to stand on. Most of the commercial weight tapes out there are inaccurate. Also, if the horse is overweight, use his ideal weight, rather than what he weighs right now. If underweight, use the current weight.

Many centers use a 20 percent formula for their able-bodied riders, and a 16 percent formula for program riders because it is much harder for a horse to carry 150 pounds of unbalanced rider, than balanced.

DIVIDE BY SIX METHOD

This formula works well to determine program rider weight, rather than able-bodied rider weight. Just divide the horse's actual weight by six to give the total weight, including rider and tack, that the horse can carry (i.e.: a 1000 pound horse can carry up to 166 pounds).

With any method, the horse's age, conformation, general health, and level of conditioning have to be considered, and the weight adjusted accordingly. It is understandable that a horse cannot carry as much weight at age twenty as he did when he was seven.

Your horse is the best indicator, however. If she begins to get cranky and you suspect her riders are on the heavy side or too unbalanced, try dropping her approved rider weight by twenty pounds. Then wait a few weeks to see if her mood and disposition improve. If so, you can gradually add weight to see where her comfort zone is. Following are additional guidelines if rider weight is a concern:

- Choose a horse with big cannon bones, wide loins, and a short back
- Avoid heavy saddles
- Have riders ride with good posture and balance
- Make sure the saddle fits the horse really well (for more information see page 92).

A few words on therapeutic driving. The average healthy horse can easily pull his own weight, but that is conditional upon having a cart or carriage with well-maintained axles and wheels. You must also consider how deep the footing is, the age and fitness of the horse, how long you ask the horse to pull, the weight of the driver(s) and the size of the wheels on the cart. When you change conditions, such as adding hills or sand, or a lot of moisture in the ground, you lower what the horse can pull.

Many programs choose to drive ponies or small horses due to the logistics of sight lines. It is hard for a volunteer on the ground to see over the top of a tall horse. If the vehicle itself is not tall, then the driver might also have trouble seeing over the horse, so it becomes a safety issue.

Anything from a miniature horse to a Haflinger or Fjord works well here, but if you are in need, always take a look at any horse who has many years of driving experience.

Therapeutic vaulting horses tend to be smaller than their able bodies counter parts, but still have wide backs, lots of bone, and an even, rhythmic stride at the walk, trot, and canter. The Haflinger does well here, too, as do small draft crosses or wide Appaloosas, Quarter Horses, and Paints.

Range of Motion 8

Flexibility is the key to a strong, well-balanced horse. Any athlete knows the benefit of stretching, bending, and flexing to improve performance, and your therapy horse is definitely an athlete. The range of motion the horse has, or how flexible he or she is, will tell you volumes about the condition of the horse's muscular and skeletal systems. If the horse can flex to one side but not the other, he could be uncomfortable when performing some mounted and unmounted tasks. Chiropractic, massage, or acupuncture may—or may not—be able to help. If he can flex very little in either direction, you may be looking at ongoing pain management. Only a qualified equine medical professional can say for sure. We'll discuss that in Chapter 17.

There are a few moves and stretches, however, that will give you a good idea of where this particular horse is with regard to movement.

HEAD AND NECK STRETCH

The poll is a control center for the mechanics of the horse's body, and several nerves in this area control the proprioception of the horse. This is where signals from nerves trigger the horse's muscles and skeleton to move a certain way. Many people don't realize how significantly this area of the horse's body governs the horse's way of going. The flexibility of

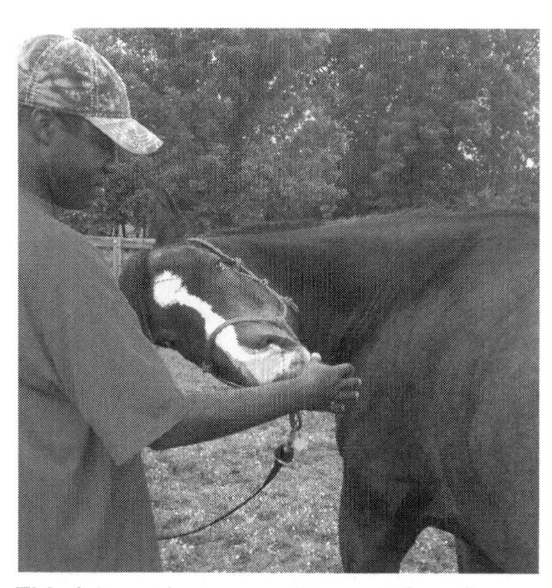

This horse shows great range of motion as he chases a carrot back to his shoulder. He was equally as limber to his right.

the poll really does determine the flexibility of the body. So, a tight poll indicates a tight horse. A loose, supple poll, one that flexes from side to side and up and down, creates loose, fluid movement throughout the horse's body.

When it comes to therapeutic riding, it is all about the movement of the horse. Whether the ride is to loosen (or tighten) human muscles or help the human mind focus, if the horse cannot move, we as facilitators lose, as does the rider.

The first stretch tests the horse's ability to move the poll and neck from side to side by gently bringing the nose back to the shoulder, and there are two ways to do this. In the first method stand on the horse's left (about a foot from the horse's ear) and face the horse. Bring your left hand around to the right side of the horse's muzzle, and gently apply pressure to encourage the horse to bring his nose to his left shoulder. You may need to help by applying gentle pressure with your right hand to the left side of the horse's neck or shoulder. The goal is to do this while the horse's legs stay planted squarely underneath him. If the horse swings his rear to the right instead of bending, stand the horse with a fence or wall next to his right side.

You may prefer the second method, but will need the owner's permission first, especially if the horse has foundered or has Cushings. Here, you stand to the left of the horse's shoulder, and hold a carrot or other treat to the left side of the horse's muzzle. Then bring the treat back to the horse's shoulder to see how hard the horse has to work to get it.

With either method, as you go through the process, you will get a sense of how easy or difficult it is for the horse to complete this movement. A younger horse should have no trouble doing this move on either side, but an older horse may have more trouble on one side than the other.

These stretches are important to do on the ground, because you will ask the horse to do them again during the test ride and it is always interesting to note if there is decreased function when the horse is carrying the weight of a rider, and if so, how much.

NOSE TO CHEST STRETCH

The nose to chest stretch tests the ability of the horse to loosen his poll up and down. Again, a carrot or treat is helpful, if the owner approves. Simply hold the treat below the horse's muzzle, and then bring it to the horse's chest.

If she does well, try again, but this time move the treat lower, to between the horse's legs at the girth area. The horse should access the treat from between her front legs, not by going around the shoulder at the side.

Remember that under the direction of a good equine medical professional, these moves and stretches can sometimes be great daily physical fitness for your horses—or not. Today they are simply an assessment tool.

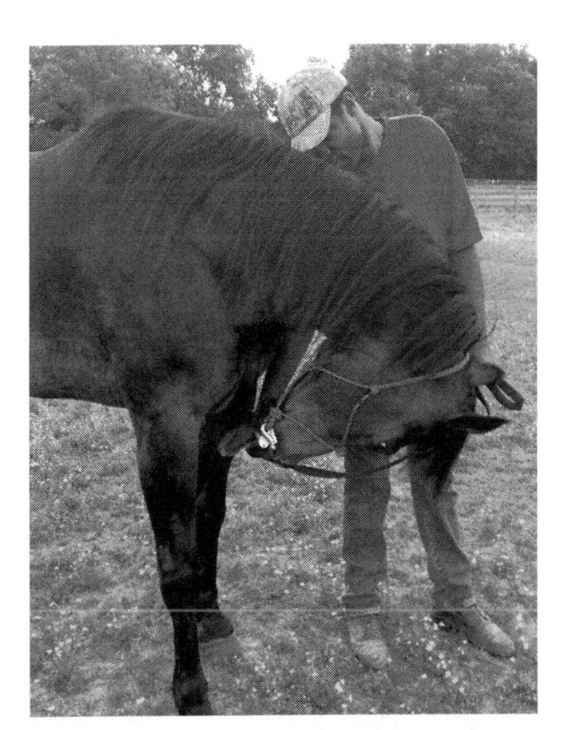

On his way to between his front legs. There is no trouble in this horse's poll.

FRONT LEG STRETCH

Leg stretches give an indication of soundness and range of motion in the limb. If for example, the prospective therapy horse has good range of motion on the left front and stretches well there, but does not want to comply when asked to do the same with the right front leg, the horse could be sore. Or, arthritis or muscle atrophy could limit the horse's range of motion. Remember that a leg stretch also involves muscles in the horse's shoulder and back, and that any limited range of motion might originate there, rather than in the leg itself.

The horse's motion is one key component that benefits your rider, if your center offers therapeutic riding. Limit the motion; limit the benefit to the rider. It is good to note here that some riders can only handle a little motion, but the movement needs to be equal on both sides and freely given from the horse, no matter what his or her natural stride. If a sore horse shortens his natural stride by six inches, it becomes an unnatural movement for that horse and translates to stiffness and tenseness throughout the horse's back and body. This stiff movement can then be jolting to the rider.

For this assessment, pick up the front leg as you would to pick out the hoof. Note the angle of the shoulder, and stretch the front leg out in front of the horse at the same angle as the shoulder. Be sure to hold the leg under the knee and fetlock. The hoof stays low to the ground. If you raise the hoof too high, you may stress joints, muscles, ligaments or tendons. If the horse resists, do not pull against him. All you need to see is if this position is comfortable, or not.

Next, move the leg back to see how far ahead of the hind foot you can place the front. Most horses cannot stretch all the way back, but see how far the horse can reach. Again, keep the foot low to the ground to avoid stress.

BACK LEG STRETCH

As with other parts of the horse, there are many stretches that can be done with the back or hind legs, and each stretch accomplishes different goals. But, the stretches you will use for evaluation are simple range of motion stretches for the purpose of assessment. This is not the time to ask the horse to stretch beyond what is comfortable.

Start by picking up a hind leg as if you were going to pick out the hoof, then gently extend the leg back and down. You will not actually stretch the leg here, just see how far back you can get it to extend. Sometimes the horse will stretch his leg back on his own, and that is always a good sign.

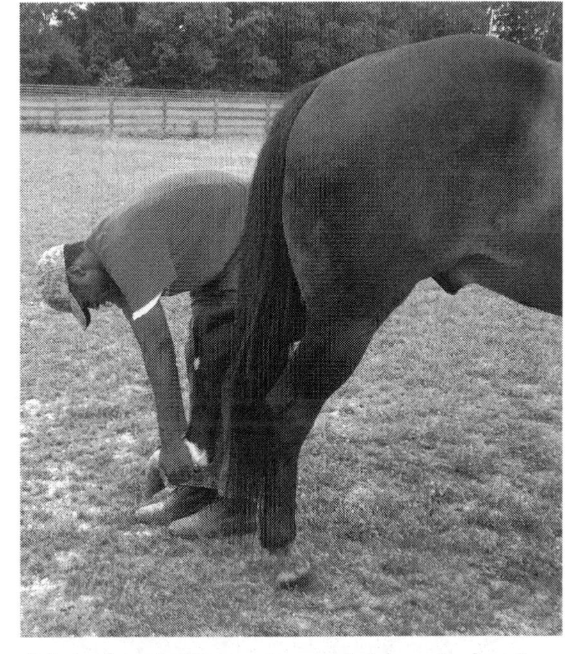

A lot of resistance was met when trying to extend the back leg. This was as far as the horse was comfortable going.

In the second stretch, hold fetlock with one hand and with your other support the leg above the hock. Gently try to bring the hind leg forward, to just behind the front leg. Many horses cannot reach nearly that far, but see how far you get. Again, be sure to keep the foot low to the ground. This is to avoid stress on the horse's soft tissue.

The third and last stretch is a diagonal hind leg stretch. Here, pick up the right hind leg from the left side, by reaching under the horse's belly. Then gently place the right hind behind the left front.

Do each stretch from both sides. What you are looking for is not how far you can move each leg, although that is important, too, but that the horse can move his hind legs equally well on both sides of his body. If you notice that one side moves significantly farther than the other, the horse might not be the best candidate as a therapeutic riding horse for people with severe physical disabilities, or as a vaulting horse, because continuous, symmetrical movement is important. The intended purpose for the horse really comes into play here.

BELLY LIFT

When the horse is asked to raise his belly, it is almost like he is asked to do a standing collection. When asked to collect under saddle, the horse has to raise his belly and lift his spine to make that happen. This move tests the ability of the horse to tighten his abdominal muscles, much as a human would do a sit up.

The importance of strong abdominal muscles translates directly to the strength of the horse's back, which correlates to rider weight and the amount of weight the horse can pull.

This mare's ear shows she is aware of her human partner. She also was able to lift her belly quite a bit.

There are several ways to ask the horse to lift his belly, but the simplest is to have one person hold the horse and another use the tips of his fingers to put upward pressure on the horse's belly near, or just behind, the girth area. Both people should note any movement when pressure is applied. The person who holds the horse can see movement, and the person who applies the pressure can feel the belly move away from the pressure of his fingers.

If there is no movement, or if the horse objects to being asked, it could be a red flag of soreness, atrophy, and/or arthritis. Not every horse will have a lot of movement here, but hopefully there will be some, or at least the horse will try.

This is also a good exercise to do daily to strengthen a horse's back and abdominals. Just a few times, though, as it is as hard for an out of shape horse to do this as it is for an out of shape human to do sit-ups.

TAIL STRETCH

Because the horse's tail is an extension of his spine, the tail stretch can benefit your horse's back. Unlike most other mammals, however, most of the horse's spine is uniquely immobile—except for the tail. The assessment of the tail is an important one, but only if you and your equine team feel it is safe to do so. If the horse is fidgety, restless, or disrespectful, or if the horse has his tail clamped between his hind legs, consider passing on this part of the evaluation.

If the horse is quiet and engaged, though, a tail stretch can tell you a lot about the status of the horse's lumbar vertebrae, and the strength and soundness of his back end. You previously observed if the tail hung straight, or if it was cocked to one side or the other. Be extra gentle with any tail manipulation if the tail was carried to the left or the right, as there might be soreness that you do not want to aggravate.

First, grasp the tail six or eight inches from the top and shake it gently. Is the tail flexible? Then gently pull the tail to the left and to the right, and note the horse's attitude. Don't pull so hard that the horse is pulled off-balance. Just apply gentle, steady pressure.

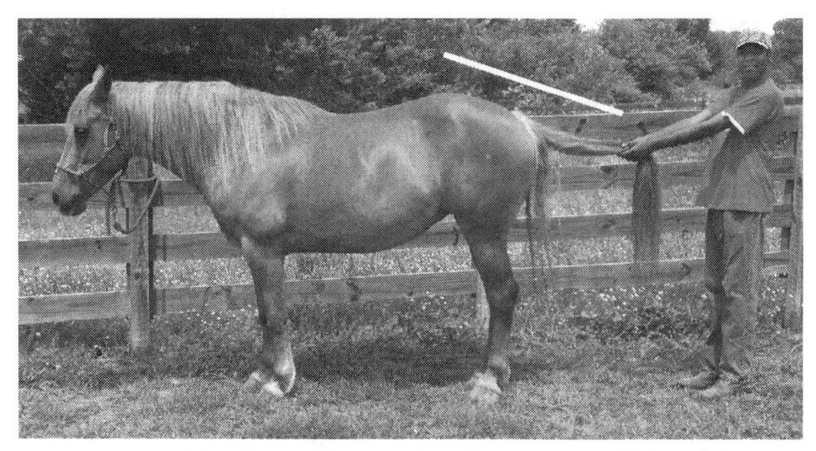

The tail should be extended to the same angle as the croup.

Then try to raise the top of the tail. Ideally, the tail will have good rotational movement, top, bottom, left, and right. If there is resistance in one direction or another, there might be arthritis or muscle tightness, or the horse's spine might be out of whack.

The last stretch is a backward one. Stand behind the horse, grasp the tail below the bone and pull outward and behind at the same angle as the croup. The horse should lean forward into this stretch while you hold it for about five seconds. The stretch decompresses the spine and temporarily adds space between the vertebrae, and we will look at this stretch again when the horse's gait is assessed in Chapter 12.

If the horse takes steps to the side, or backs up to relieve the pressure, think about soreness somewhere in the spine. Soreness has been mentioned a lot and most horses, like many people, have some. It is the degree of soreness that matters. If there is only mild soreness on the left shoulder and along the left side of the back, maybe it can be worked out with massage. If, however, the horse is moderately to severely sore over a half dozen areas of his body, it complicates matters. Even if the horse only plays a part in your ground lessons, if he is sore enough that when a participant bumps the sore area that he snaps, it becomes a matter of safety.

HEAD DROP / POLL RELEASE

The poll release is not a stretch, but checks the horse's willingness to accept you as his or her leader. It's done here, rather than earlier, because you and your team have now worked with the horse enough to establish some leadership.

It's an easy enough exercise with two ways of going about it, and is a good way to also get an indication where the horse may be positioned in your herd. If the horses at your center are turned out, you will want a good mix in your herd of leaders, middle rankers, and followers. Horses always seem to work these things out, but if you have two herd leaders who continually challenge each other it can become a safety issue for volunteers who need to go into the pasture to bring a horse in for a lesson.

On the other hand, a horse who is continually at the bottom of the pecking order may not have enough confidence in himself to be a great therapy horse, or he may have a great deal of confidence and instead choose to stay out of the drama at the bottom of the herd.

In any case, if a horse submits to pressure on the poll and drops her head, it shows that she is willing to work with you. Some herd leaders, especially mares, will rarely drop, and certainly not for someone she has just met. From a horse's perspective, it is about being safe. In the wild, a bobcat or another predator might jump out of

This lead mare will drop her head only for a select few—people she has known and trusted for a long time.

a tree or over a small cliff to land on the horse's most vulnerable spot, the poll. It is one of the few areas of the horse's body that the horse cannot see (or reach with her teeth), and close enough to the jugular vein that a predator can reach down to it in seconds. If the horse feels you are competent enough to defend her from a bobcat attack, then she will drop her head. If not, she will resist. It is as simple as that.

The first way to ask a horse to drop her head, assuming the horse is haltered, is to put downward pressure on the lead rope. If, after a second or two the horse does not respond, the human doing the asking should release the pressure, then ask again while bending forward at the waist.

The desired result can be anything from a lowering of the head and neck a few inches, to your prospective horse putting her nose to the ground. It may be, however, that your horse resists, and pulls away from the pressure. This horse is not yet ready to give leadership to you and this result is very common in lead mares.

The second way to ask a horse to drop her head is the preferred method of many, and that is simply to apply pressure with your fingertips to the poll area. Success, however, depends on the horse/human height ratio. If the human is short and the horse is tall, it may be awkward (or even impossible) to apply fingertip pressure at the poll. In that event, the first method is safer.

If there will be a lot of people working with the horse and the horse does not drop her head during the assessment, it may be that she will challenge each new leader or handler. The amount of testing may be small, or the horse may be very difficult for new people to work with. One lead mare I worked with allowed me leadership only after a year of working with her. She had a rough start with some tough training methods and it took her that long to trust, although she made an excellent therapy horse at a small center with few volunteers long before then.

Overall, age makes a big difference in a horse's flexibility and that should be taken into consideration as you write down your comments on the assessment form. The average six-year-old horse will have more flex than a sixteen-year-old. In addition, your assessment is not about pushing the horse out of his or her comfort zone, but in finding what range of motion is easily reached.

Temperament and Personality 9

The temperament and personality of the horse is critical to success in a therapy program. Even if you are in search of a horse for an able-bodied intermediate adult rider of his or her own, the temperament and personality have to fit the person who will handle the horse most often. And that, in a therapy center, is a challenge.

In some programs, a horse is handled by ten or more people a day. Some of the people handling the horse might be volunteers who are not horse people, and who know little about the ways of the horse. Others might be program participants who have physical, cognitive, or emotional challenges. And then there are all the human personalities that make up the center's staff and instructors.

It takes a very special horse to be willing and respectful to all of those people. While you won't know for sure if the horse you look at today will soon be your center's newest superstar, one way to get a glimpse into the future is to have every member of your team work and interact with the horse during your visit. Then take note how the horse reacts to each human personality.

This is another area where it will come in handy to know exactly why you need the horse. Many think a therapy horse needs to be a quiet, settled horse, but that is not always true. If your center does ground work, for example, with veterans who have Post Traumatic Stress Disorder (PTSD), then having one horse who is a little on the "up" or nervous side, or who does not engage well with people, might be a horse your clientele can really relate to.

Also of huge importance is the personality of the horse. Does he seem interested in all of the people who have come to see him? Or, is he bored to tears? Does he lean in for scratches and hugs, or ignore you? Some engagement is always nice. Program participants often relate better to a horse who shows interest in them, and because of that interest, the participants progress faster.

A horse who tunes out people can quickly become disenchanted with his new job. And, from a safety standpoint, a horse who is not engaged in the activities around him may become startled when something out of the ordinary happens. Or, he may become so displeased that he behaves poorly. Like some people, some horses just do not like their job. Of course, it is possible that the disengaged horse you visit today might not like his current job and will perk up once he arrives at your center. For some things, only time will tell.

While engagement is good, the horse also needs to be polite, stand still when asked, and not invade his handler's personal space. Many horses who live with an individual person have sloppy manners, only because the human partner allows it. Once the horse is told what the new rules are, most are happy to comply.

I have worked with several therapy horses, though, who always pushed the boundaries. If the handler gave an inch, each horse took a mile. Even though these big personality horses were huge challenges, each center surrounded their horse with experienced handlers and each horse became a fabulous therapy horse who was at his respective center for many years.

These horses do need special handling, though. Does your center have a trainer who can teach the horse the new rules? And, do you have enough experienced people on staff or in your volunteer base to keep the horse reminded of those rules? If so, you may be in for a treat—or it could be a nightmare.

For therapeutic riding, driving, or vaulting, the horse should be on the quiet, respectful side. Even if you need a horse who can walk, trot, and canter with your clients independently, for reasons of safety, the horse should be quiet in nature.

I looked at a newly-retired polo pony a few years ago and while she was willing and respectful, I got the sense that, given the opportunity, she would gladly race across the field with me aboard. Of course, that was what she was trained to do; that had been her job for many years.

Everything else about the horse checked out very well, though, so we took her on. She ended up being one of the best therapeutic riding horses I ever worked with. She had an innate ability to determine exactly what each rider needed and became a "go to" horse for independent walk-trot riders. When a person with a disability rode, her head was low, her eye soft, her tail long and loose. When a staff member or other able-bodied person got on, however, this mare could be a handful.

Intelligent, sensible, intuitive, helpful equines make the best therapy horses. If your team collectively feels you are looking at one of these, it is hard to not at least give her a try. One way to test for those traits is to offer a series of toys and exercises to see how the horse responds.

A horse who is curious, and who explores or plays with new objects, is engaged and interested in his surroundings.

Start with a small washcloth or plastic grocery bag that you have brought with you. Let the horse smell it, then rub it over her body, both left and right sides. While doing this, note any area you touch where she pins her ears. Then open up the bag or cloth and with an underhand motion, slowly toss the object along her neck, legs, belly, and flank. Be sure to keep your body posture neutral. Note her reaction and if she gets excited or anxious, back off. This is not a desensitizing session; you are just checking her reaction.

Next bring out a small nerf ball or stuffed animal. Let her smell the object, then gently toss it along her neck, sides, and flank, and on the ground in front of her and to her sides. This is not about trying to scare the horse, but to assess her reaction to unusual objects and situations. Repeat the process with bells, or some other object that makes noise.

Horses who show curiosity about an object often make good therapy horses, either on the ground or under saddle. Their curiosity shows that the horse is open to new things and has enough self-confidence to take small risks.

By this time you should have enough information about the horse's personality to move to the next step.

Overall Health 10

During your assessment of all of the horse's body parts and movement, you should also assess the horse's general health, and with a little practice this is easy to do.

EYE

One of the first things to look at is the eye. Does the horse have a dull eye that might indicate physical or emotional pain? Or, is the eye bright and engaged?

Blindness is also a consideration and sometimes it is hard to tell how good a horse's vision actually is. You can wave your hand two or three feet in front of the horse's eye to see if the horse responds with a head toss or a blink, but a placid, comfortable horse many not react, even if she sees you very clearly. A veterinarian can always check the horse's quality of vision during the vet check (see Chapter 17), if you get that far with this particular horse.

Some horses will have an eye that is misshapen by an injury, or he or she may have been born with a malformed eye. As a rule, horses who do not have good vision do not do well going into therapy programs, although horses who start with good vision and gradually lose it during their time at a center often adapt well. There are exceptions to every rule, though, so it is good to keep an open mind until your entire assessment is complete.

SKIN

The next area to check is the skin. The skin is more important than it looks, as it protects the inside of the horse's body from rain, wind, dirt, and all sorts of contamination, and also helps maintain the horse's internal body temperature.

With a quick spot check, look for dry scaly patches and open sores. Poor skin can be an indication of many things, including flies, poor nutrition, or lack of grooming. Those are simple matters to correct, however, worms, fungus, allergies, liver disease, or other illness that causes skin problems may require more intensive work to remedy.

This is also a good time to check the horse for lumps and bumps that might be tumors. White and gray horses are especially prone to melanomas, which may or may not be malignant. These tumors can appear as spots or patches, or raised or flat masses. Most have a dark surface, and can cluster around the eye, or the base of the tail.

HAIR

A glossy coat of hair is a sign of a healthy horse. Fortunately, most horses have this. It is the horses who don't that you need to look at more closely.

Is the horse missing patches of hair? This horse may be low on the totem pole and be regularly beaten up by other members of the herd. Or, the horse could have an allergy and be scratching the hair away. Gnats could be an issue here, too, as they can cause patchy hair loss in the summer. Lice, mange, urine or manure scald, rain scald, ringworm (which is a fungus), too much selenium, or even sarcoid skin tumors can also cause hair loss.

Sarcoids usually affect younger horses, but can be infective from one horse to the other. If you suspect that your horse prospect has these, do not bring the horse onto your property until a veterinarian has given the horse the all clear. Most of the other conditions mentioned are simple environmental fixes.

What about dull or coarse hair? Think poor nutrition, or nutrition that is out of balance with regard to fats, carbohydrates, and/or proteins.

Parasites or a systemic infection also come to mind in horses with a dull hair coat. Allergies or hormones could factor in, too. Or, maybe the horse just needs a good bath.

If the horse's hair is exceptionally long and it is not the middle of winter, Cushings could be the cause. The Cushinoid horse may still make an excellent therapy horse, but will need special care, including a dry lot as fresh grass can, in some cases, be deadly.

WEIGHT

Like people, some horses by nature are thinner or heavier. A Thoroughbred, for example, may always be on the lean side, no matter how many calories you try to stuff into her. Haflingers, Fjords, and some pony breeds are always on the heavy side. It's as if they gain weight on the air they breathe.

A horse's weight comes into play in two areas during an assessment. The first is an estimation of the horse's optimal weight with regard to the weight of any program rider who might ride the horse. If a 14.3 hand horse's current weight is 1100 pounds, but you estimate the horse ideally should weigh 900 pounds, she may not be the horse you need for a veteran's program, as the horse will be limited to lighter weight riders.

The second area where weight comes into play during an assessment is if the horse is overly fat or thin. Thank goodness that heavier horses are more common than thin ones, but those who are heavy might not be so from too much food. In addition to Cushings, hormones, breed type, or lack of exercise may be the cause.

If it looks as if the very thin horse has adequate feed, there could be many variables that keep the horse from gaining weight. Hormones make this list, too, as do parasites, systemic infection, gastric ulcers, stress, and breed type. But, dental issues top the list.

A horse has to chew food thoroughly if he is to digest it completely. If his teeth have been neglected, he might not be able to chew properly. A sharp point on a tooth, a tooth that is infected, or an oral abscess can also cause discomfort and make a horse hesitant to eat. Only an equine dentist or DVM can let you know for sure if this horse has dental problems.

DEMEANOR

Finally, a good look at the horse's demeanor will tell you a lot. Is he engaged with people? Curious? Willing? Pleasant? Do the horse's ears move back and forth? Is the tail carried loosely?

Or, do the horse's ears flatten often? Does the horse seem cranky? Has he tried to kick? Does he clamp his tail or swish it in anger? Does he balk when asked to move?

There are so many possible factors here that it would be impossible to go into all of them. But, if the horse does not seem willing and happy, there's most likely a problem that you do not want to tackle. Most centers are so safety conscious that bringing an ill-tempered horse into the program, no matter what the cause, is a huge risk.

Leading and Soundness 11

Leading and soundness are evaluated together because one can't be evaluated without the other. Leading refers to how well the horse leads, and being sound means that the horse is without a lameness that would make the horse unfit for normal use. As a correlation, many people have bad knees and have no trouble walking a mile, but are gimpy enough at a jog to be considered unsound.

LEADING

Horses are trained with different methods by different people, especially for groundwork. Some horses are asked to follow his or her human leader, while others are trained to keep their eye or ear near the human's shoulder. Some horses mosey on along somewhere in between.

To assess the horse's leading skills, take into consideration how the horse has been trained. It is unfair to evaluate a horse based on one method when her training has been in another. What is important is the horse's willingness to please you and her ability to follow directions, even if they are directions that are new to her.

Most centers ask horses to lead by keeping their eye or ear next to the human's shoulder. This is for safety. It is important for the leader to see the horse, and much can be determined about the state of the horse's mind if the leader can see the horse's ear, eye, and mouth. In therapeutic riding, the leader also has more control over the horse if the horse is next to the leader, versus behind. However, each center or program does things differently. There is no right or wrong way, as long it is a safe way and consistently follows center procedure.

During the assessment, the horse should be asked to lead at the walk and trot from both the left and right sides. It is not uncommon for horses to be a little sticky on the right side, as most are rarely led that way. What you do not want to see is pinned ears or snappy teeth when asked to lead from either side.

The horse should be asked to do walk/trot, walk/halt, trot/walk, and trot/halt transitions, and to walk and trot around left and right corners when led from both directions. In an ideal situation the horse will stay with the leader on a loose lead, but not rush ahead. The horse will easily increase and decrease speed, turn, and stop. Most horses were originally trained to lead correctly, whether at the shoulder or following behind, but many owners get sloppy with cues and corrections, and so a horse's leading skills can deteriorate over time. That's why the willingness of the horse to cooperate is so important, rather than the current level of the skill.

If I have one suggestion for an owner who wants to donate a horse to a center, it is to brush up on the horse's leading skills. No matter what activities the center offers, it almost always involves leading. And, a horse who leads exceptionally well will definitely score extra points during an assessment.

The horse should also be asked to back. This is where some horses refuse. It may be because the horse has not been asked to back recently, and that's not an awful thing, as it is not difficult to teach a horse to back from the ground.

If, however, the horse refuses to back because it is painful for her to do so, you might take another look at the back, lumbar vertebrae, hips, stifle and hocks. Some programs do not ask their older horses to back at all. But, the horse should try to back when asked.

This is a good time, too, to ask the horse to disengage her hips. To do this, stand near the horse's hip, then either twirl the end of the lead rope, or press on the barrel or horse's flank. Different natural horsemanship trainers teach this in slightly different ways, but the horse usually gets the idea. Watch for the horse to cross one hind leg in front of the other, to move away from the cue. Then ask the horse to stop. This crossing of legs also indicates that the horse is physically able to do so. Some stiff horses will bring one leg next to the other, then move the other leg away, rather than crossing over with the first leg.

When you finish on the left side, do the same on the right. Two things should be apparent. One is the willingness of the horse to do this. There is a saying that if you can control the horse's hindquarters, you can control the horse's mind. A horse who easily moves her hindquarters when asked should be a respectful, willing horse.

The second is whether the ease of movement is equal on both sides. If there is resistance on one or both sides, the horse might be sore or have arthritis severe enough that it is painful to move in this manner. Sometimes it is a fine line in determining the difference between pain and disrespect, so your entire team should watch closely.

LAMENESS VS. SOUNDNESS

The terms lameness and soundness (or unsoundness) are often used interchangeably, but some people are more comfortable with a subtle difference. Depending on which person you talk to, a lameness might be recent, temporary, or something the horse is currently undergoing treatment for, while an unsoundness is a long-term, chronic condition. Others will say that a lameness is due to an injury, while an unsoundness is structural, and caused by poor conformation, poor bone structure, or weak muscles.

Regardless, if the horse you have gone to look at does not move in a rhythmic, even gait, or is obviously in pain, try to figure out why, as the "why" can often tell you if it is a fixable problem.

Soundness (or lameness) can be difficult to evaluate, and for many reasons. One, there are varying degrees of soundness. There is "perfectly sound," "serviceably sound," and "definitely lame." Perfectly sound translates to: based on the evaluation today, the horse will probably hold up for most reasonable uses. Serviceably sound means the horse will most likely be okay for some light work. Lame means just that. It is painful for the horse to move forward and there is a noticeable deviation in the gait as a result.

Another reason an unsoundness might be difficult to diagnose is if the horse is gaited or normally has an unusual way of going, or if the horse has poor conformation, but has figured out a way to get from point A to point B that is different from other horses, but usual for this one. Whether the problem is in the shoulder, hip, hoof, hock, stifle or any other place on the horse's body can also be tough to determine. Sometimes only a skilled diagnostician can determine the true cause of the problem, and where it is.

Should a lameness or unsoundness be a red flag for your program? Maybe. It depends on how you expect the horse to fit into your center, the probable cause of the problem, and whether or not good care can improve matters. Only you and your team can decide if it is worth the risk.

We will discuss more about the actual gait itself in Chapter 12, and soundness certainly is a part of the horse's gait. But here we'll concentrate on the issues that might prevent a prospective horse from entering your program. This is another subject where entire books have been written, so we'll only go into the most basic movements that you might see. If, however, you suspect something is not right, and if you decide to take the horse on trial, be sure to mention your thoughts to your veterinarian and farrier (or trimmer) before the pre-donation or pre-purchase exams.

Front-end lameness often is the easiest to see. Just as you might wince when putting a sore foot on the ground, so does your horse. Watch the horse as he is walked and trotted in a straight line on a loose lead over firm, even ground. Usually, a horse will raise his head when weight bearing on a sore front limb. Or, you might notice the horse drop his head when the sound leg hits the ground. In either case, the horse's head and neck will be higher whenever the ouchy limb becomes weight bearing. This is true whether at the walk, or at the trot or gait.

Rear-end lamenesses can be harder for some people to spot, but generally, if the lameness is in the rear, the horse will drop his hip on the side that is lame. That's why it often is easiest to spot a rear lameness by looking at the horse's hip, or rear topline, rather than at his feet or legs.

On the off chance that the horse is unsound on both front or both rear legs, there will be little to no head or hip raising or lowering. But, the horse's strides will be short and choppy, and the horse may, understandably, be cranky or unwilling.

If you think the horse is off, look for the injury from the ground up while the horse is standing still. If he rests one leg continually, or avoids placing weight on a leg, that's a good indication the limb is sore—somewhere. You can check for heat or swelling, although you may not find either. Then pick up the hoof. Stone bruises or tender soles after a trim, or even rocky terrain, can cause a horse to be ouchy. Moving up the leg and into the shoulder or hip, there can be any number of muscle strains or other injuries. It is not up to you to diagnose, but if you can get a probable cause it can help with your assessment and selection.

Sometimes the horse owner is unaware that the horse has a problem. It's best to tread lightly at first to test the owner's emotional response to the news that her horse is lame, and then suggest that an equine medical professional be called. Even though you care, you do not want to offer a diagnosis or treatment, even if it comes out of concern. There may be liability issues involved if the lameness turns out to be something other than what you think it is, or if your suggested course of action does not improve the horse's condition.

Taking video footage of the horse as he moves can help you see exactly what, if anything, is going on. If the horse is definitely sore, you should not continue the assessment. But, if the horse is promising in other ways, leave the door open with his owner and ask her to call you when the problem has been resolved.

Gait 12

If you offer hippotherapy, therapeutic riding, or therapeutic vaulting, the actual gait, or movement, of the horse is of paramount importance, as it also is to some extent in therapeutic driving. The movement of the horse really is quite magical and while all horses move their legs in the same sequence when they walk, trot or gait, and canter, no two horses have exactly the same movement.

Even if you only do groundwork, the gait of the horse can come into play if the horse's stride is exceptionally long or short, fast or slow. I know of one center that has a contract with a local senior center. Twice a week the seniors come out to take horses for walks. This helps these older people get exercise, be more social, interact with people outside the center, and learn leadership through the ways of the horse. What a wonderful opportunity for all involved!

The center, however, cannot use some of their horses in this wonderful program. Large, leggy Thoroughbreds or Warmbloods, long-striding gaited horses, and energetic horses who walk very fast are unsuitable because the seniors cannot keep up. The same might also be the case if your program has younger children or people with a physical disability who lead horses. The center with the senior program often looks for horses who have short strides at both the walk and the trot, and typically adds new horses that are ponies, Quarter Horses, Appaloosas, or Paints who walk slowly and can almost jog in place.

In addition to the speed and length of stride, there are many other factors to look for in assessing a horse's gait. The first to look for is tracking. Here, you will look for two things: the distance the horse covers with each stride, and the straightness of the track.

The distance, or length of stride, will depend on the horse's breed, build, and level of physical fitness. It makes sense that a horse with long legs and a short back (think tall rectangle) will have a longer stride than a horse with a long back and short legs (long rectangle). Typically, the longer the stride the more movement the rider gets at the walk. While there are exceptions to the rule, if very little movement for physically fragile riders is needed, look for a horse with a short, but smooth stride.

In therapeutic riding movement is an integral benefit, so many programs look for horses with a lot of movement. The horse's movement either rocks the rider's pelvis back and forth, from side to side, in a figure eight motion, or a combination of all three. Big movement helps a rider focus and provides good physical benefits.

To get that level of movement the height ratio of withers to hip comes into play. If the horse's hip is taller than the withers, then powerful hindquarter muscles can better push the left and right sides of the rider's pelvis forward. This movement from the horse pushes the human rider's body into a simulation of pelvic movement at the walk, and is excellent for riders who are unsteady on their feet, or wheelchair bound.

If the hip is too much higher, though, the upward slant of the horse's back may tip the rider's upper body forward. The same problem exists in reverse if the horse's withers are significantly higher than the horse's hip. In this instance the tilt of the horse's topline could tip the rider back. As they say, balance in all things!

THE WALK

One major component of gait to look for on the ground is the horse's ability to overtrack. Overtracking is the amount of distance the horse's back hoof over steps the horse's front hoof at the walk. To see this, have a team member lead the horse at a medium walk in a straight line. First, watch where the horse lands her front feet, then watch to see if the horse's hind feet fall short of the front imprint, land on top of it, or land in front of it. These three options are called undertracking, tracking up, and overtracking. Depending on how fast the horse is being led, some horses can do all three—just not at the same time.

The sequence of the horse's stride at the walk is left hind, left front, right hind, and right front. In this way, the walk is a lateral gait. Left, left, right, right. The important consideration is how far underneath herself the horse can reach with her back legs. A horse who overtracks usually gives good movement. Overtracking is also often a sign of a horse who is free of arthritis or soreness. The horse's build, however has to be taken into consideration. A horse with a long body and short legs may also be free of arthritis and soreness, even though it is physically impossible for her to reach underneath herself as far as a leggy Warmblood can.

Another consideration to look for is whether the horse tracks up evenly on the left and right sides. Tracking differently left and right is quite common in horses who have suffered an injury, or who have overused a specific joint. The result is an uneven gait for the rider. Rather than an even push left and right from the hind legs, there could be a big push from the left hind, and a medium push from the right hind. The horse then makes up for the lack of distance from the right hind with a larger stride from the right front.

As you can imagine, for a physically fragile rider this kind of gait could aggravate weak muscles and joints, rather than strengthen them. Also, if you teach ground driving or vaulting, or ask participants or volunteers to walk in rhythm with the horse's legs, an uneven rhythm such as this could be frustrating, rather than empowering.

Something else to look for is if the horse's back legs follow in the same track, or path, as the front. To see this, stand behind the horse while a committee member leads him in a straight line away from you. Some horses who have back problems will land their back feet to the left or right of where the front feet land. Often, you can let your eye travel up to the horses topline and see that the horse's hips and lower spine are also canted to the left or right.

Once you have noted the horse's tracking at the walk, have your handler lead the horse away from you at the trot and note if there is a difference in tracking from the walk.

While you are standing behind the horse, also look to see if the hocks wobble in or out at either the walk or trot. Wobbly hocks can be a sign of soreness or weakness in the joint, and either can affect the horse's way of going, and how much work he can handle.

THE TROT

While the walk is a lateral gait, at the trot the horse moves his legs in diagonal pairs. Left hind and right front move forward together, then the right hind and left front. If the horse is moving fast enough and is balanced, there may be a period of suspension between the strides where all of the horse's legs are off the ground.

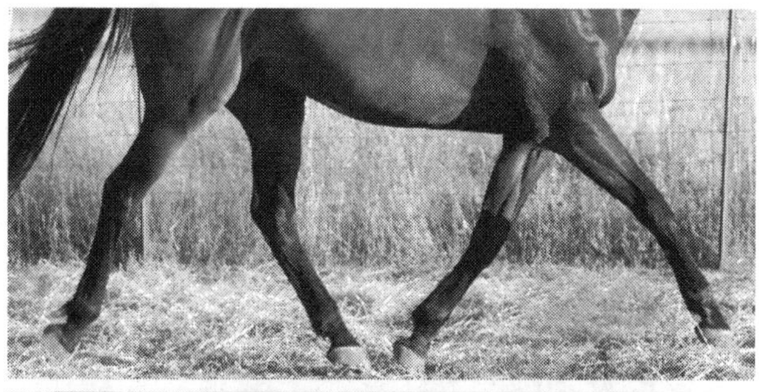

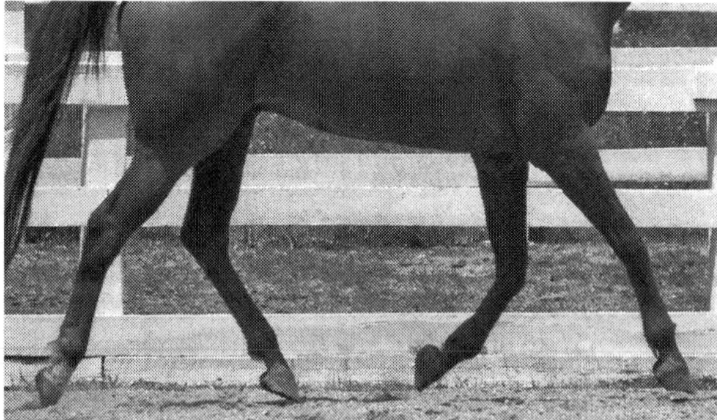

While both horses are trotting at about the same speed, it is easy to see that the horse in the top photo has a longer stride. The horse reaches farther forward with his front leg, and the distance between the front and back legs under the belly is much shorter than with the horse in the bottom photo.

Stride length also plays a factor. Horses with big knee and hock action, such as the Hackney Pony, Saddlebred, and other such breeds, can have a big bounce to their trot, but the stride will be short. Instead of length, these horses use up their motion in knee and hock height.

A Thoroughbred, or even a breedy Quarter Horse will have a long, low reach to her stride. Here, wither and hip height will determine how smooth the gait is to ride. Going back to conformation, even the height the neck is carried will have a factor on the horse's gait. High necks indicate more knee and hock lift than a horse who carries her neck lower.

GAITED HORSES

Most gaited horses, with the exception of the Peruvian Paso, Paso Fino and one or two others, have a very long stride. Some centers like this, as a gaited walk provides a lot of movement, and movement can strengthen a rider's core and develop focus. Other centers that have many riders who need one or two sidewalkers find their volunteers cannot keep up with a big-strided walk.

Gaited horses usually overtrack well at the walk and if the movement is slow enough, or the horse is small enough, these horses can be a good choice. The gaited horse is also good for a rider who, for whatever reason, is not a good candidate to learn a post trot. Not posting can be limiting, though, for riders who *could* learn that skill. Many gaited horses also do not gait consistently. One Tennessee Walking Horse I work with gaits in a nice consistent manner with an experienced rider, but with program participants, sometimes trots, sometimes paces, and other times performs a nice running walk. This makes difficult any activity that needs consistency in the gait.

THE CANTER

Not all centers have riders who are independent enough to canter, but many do. Cantering is a skill many more riders at therapeutic centers could master, if only they had a horse who could help teach them how.

I like to see a horse canter without a rider, even if I do not expect to have the horse canter during program activities. A good, balanced, even canter on both left and right leads is yet another indication of a horse whose muscles, bones, and joints are healthy.

Even if the horse has a good canter, she might not be suitable for canter activities at your center. Vaulters need a larger horse with a wide back, so a small, narrow horse would probably not work well. A rider who is just learning to canter needs a horse with a calm temperament, and a slow gait. The horse also needs to be willing to respond to cues that are close to being exact. There is nothing more frustrating than a rider who is trying hard and coming close, yet getting no positive results from the horse.

The horse also needs to go into an easy canter from a walk or slow trot, keep cantering without the rider having to thump her with strong legs every stride, and drift slowly back to a walk when asked. If you find such a horse offered as a donation to your center, one that is sound, know they are very rare. While there may be other considerations that will make you pass, before you do, think of the current and future needs of your program. If you have riders who can, say, in the next six to twelve months benefit from a horse who canters, if that's all the horse brings to your program, you may want to consider her.

Those horses, however, who have unusual variations in gait, may be the same horses who had a stiff or sensitive tail during the tail assessment, or who carried a tail left or right of center. A free moving, centered tail, usually means free, flowing gaits.

The Ride 13

We've talked about safety and it pops up again here. For reasons of safety it is a good idea to have the current owner, or someone who knows the horse, ride him before you do. In fact, before you visit, be sure that whoever shows the horse to you knows of this expectation and if he or she cannot ride the horse, that they have someone there who can.

Having someone else ride before you do accomplishes two purposes. One, you have better assurance that the horse is safe for you or one of your committee members to get on, and two, you can do a quick assessment of the horse under saddle. Does the horse seem willing to go forward, or are his ears pinned and his tail swishing? Does the horse still overtrack at a good working walk evenly both left and right? Does the horse still carry his tail evenly between his butt cheeks, or is it now carried to one side? Are any of the other assessments you did without a rider more pronounced or different with a rider? It is very possible that you will see some differences, for carrying the weight of a rider can change much of what you observed on the ground.

The demonstration rider's weight, height, and skill also have to be taken into account, as does the fit of the saddle. If the demonstration rider is too heavy for the horse, or a poor rider who pulls on the reins or digs her heels into the horse's sides, then it is understandable that the horse might be cranky or unwilling.

You will want the owner or demo rider to walk, trot, canter, turn, stop, and back up. A long ride is not necessary. In three to five minutes you can usually see whether or not the horse is safe, willing, and sound.

SADDLE FIT

As a guess, about 90 percent of riders who participate in my clinics arrive with saddles that do not fit their horse. This is critical, because poor saddle fit nearly always causes the horse to become sore. During an assessment, if you find the saddle does not fit and the horse is grumpy, this may be the reason. With a few weeks rest to allow time for the soreness to go away, and to find a better fitting saddle, this horse still might be a good candidate for your program. Massage, acupuncture, and chiropractic work can speed up the healing process.

A master saddle fitter can give details about getting a good fit, but basic information can give an indication of a bad fit for either an English or a western saddle. When looking for a good fit, have the horse stand squarely on all four legs and then place the saddle on the horse's back—without a pad. Here are a few things to look for:

1. If your fingers are pinched and uncomfortable when you slide them between the horse's shoulder and the front of the saddle, the fit is too tight.

2. If you do not have at least several inches of clearance between the horse's withers and the underside of the pommel (the front) of the saddle, the front of the saddle is too wide.

3. If the seat tilts forward or back, the saddle does not fit. A backward tilt usually means the saddle is too tight or the withers are too high and a forward tilt the saddle is too loose or the horse has very high hips, although there are variations on this.

4. If the back of the saddle does not make continuous contact with the horse it will flop up and down when the horse moves and be uncomfortable for the horse to wear. Also be sure on a western saddle that the back of the saddle does not bend downward and dig into the horse.

5. On a western saddle, be sure the skirt does not rub the area between the horse's hip and stifle. This sometimes happens on short backed horses who wear a western saddle with a square skirt.

6. The underside of the center of any saddle should lie flat and not "bridge" away from the horse. You can check this under the stirrup area.

7. Be sure the groove on the underside of the saddle is wide enough for the horse's spine and does not pinch the spine.

Your role here is not to give the owner a lesson on saddle fit, but understand why their horse might not perform to expectation. If the horse is unwilling and you also know the saddle is uncomfortable for the horse to wear, you then have to determine if the horse's attitude will improve once you get him to your center and find a saddle that fits. A good educated guess is all that is really possible for now. The horse will tell you for sure if and when you bring him to your facility.

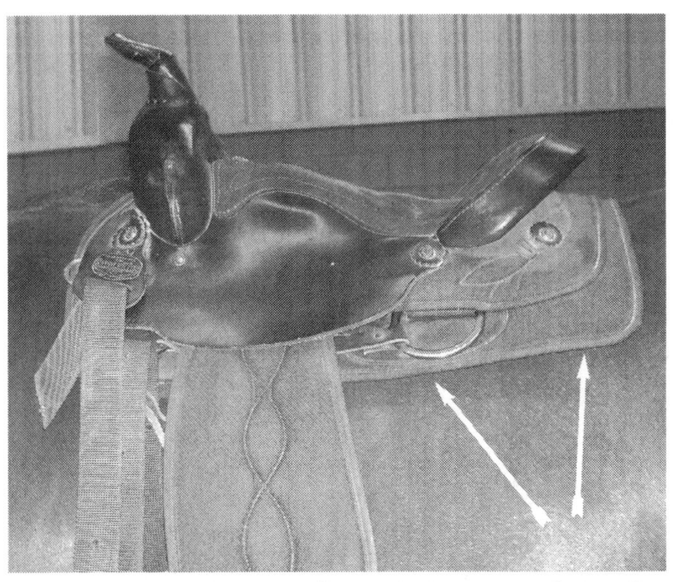

This western saddle lies flat and shows no signs of bridging. There is adequate clearance between the wither and pommel, and the seat is level enough to provide a balanced ride for the rider.

SAFETY

In addition to the owner riding first, for safety, be sure the footing of your riding area is appropriate for the assessment. Twice, I have arrived to look at a horse for a therapeutic program only to realize, due to muddy, rocky, or uneven footing, that the only riding assessment we could do was at the walk. Both horses passed the initial on-site assessment, but when they were brought to the center, unsoundness issues were seen when the horses were asked to trot under saddle. Sadly, both horses had to go home.

If you can only do a walk assessment under saddle, that's all you can do. Safety for horse and rider are paramount. Just know that you may find unforeseen problems when you get the horse to your location. It's a risk, however, that many programs choose to take, especially if the horse seems suitable on most other accounts.

Also, if for any reason you or any member of your team feels unsafe at any point in the assessment, stop. There is always risk when you interact with a horse and that risk increases when it is a horse you do not know at someone else's farm.

THE RIDER

It is important that the person on your team who rides the horse is height and weight appropriate for the horse's height and weight. It would be unfair to the horse to try to evaluate him if he is 14 hands, and the rider is six feet tall and weighs two hundred pounds. If you are evaluating a pony, bring along the child of a team member or small adult friend, as long as the rider is knowledgeable. It (almost) goes without saying that you should never ask any rider to get on a horse or pony unless you are confident that he or she will be safe.

In an ideal world, the rider should be skilled enough to give you the "feel" of the horse. How willing, sensitive, well-trained is the horse? A good rider can determine what training the horse has, and what advanced movements, if any, the horse has been taught.

There are some schools of thought that a highly trained horse is never suitable for a mounted therapy program, because an off-balance rider could unintentionally give a cue for a canter. With some horses that may be true. However, a good, intuitive horse who tries hard to please somehow knows the difference between a trained able-bodied rider and one who has a disability.

I have worked with several third level dressage horses, as well as a retired grand-prix jumper, who all made very good mounted therapy horses—as have an award-winning, push-button western pleasure horse; a top polo pony; and many other horses who were well-educated.

For unmounted lessons I actually prefer a horse with a higher education. A horse who respectfully moves his hips when asked or backs easily is an amazing asset to your program. A horse who can sidepass over a ground pole with instructions from a program participant on the ground, or perform a 360 degree turn in a box made of poles, or weave cones on a long lead held by the same participant is worth his weight in gold.

THE MOUNT

Helmets please! Many freak accidents can happen when riding a horse and a helmet can minimize or even prevent injury, so be sure your rider has brought a helmet along—one that fits.

Hopefully your rider will be able to mount from a mounting block, but not every owner or facility has one. It puts a lot of torque on a horse's back when a rider, especially a heavy one, mounts from the ground. Over time, this continual twisting of the muscles of the horse's topline and sides can cause soreness, or even arthritis. If there is not a block available, or you do not have a portable one to bring with you, a good leg up will suffice.

Years ago a riding instructor told me that if I could not get on my horse without a girth or cinch, and without the saddle slipping, then I either needed to learn how to do that, or mount with the assistance of a block or a leg up. That is still good advice today, although I wouldn't ever suggest trying to mount a horse you have just gone to see without a girth.

There are many specifics to look for during the mount. When the rider gets on, does the horse pin his ears or try to bite or snap at the rider?

Swish his tail? Move his rear away from the mounting block or the rider, or not stand still? Does he walk off as soon as the rider gets on, or does he respectfully stand until the rider asks him to move forward? With the exception of biting, tail swishing, and ear pinning, all of which can indicate either soreness or the expectation of soreness, the other negative behaviors are often the result of sloppy owner training. The owner has not enforced the good habits the horse learned when he was initially trained and as a result, has developed bad habits. These usually go away with continued reinforcement of good behavior.

FLEXION

After the mount, ask the horse to walk away a few steps, and then stop. This accomplishes two things: you can tell how well the horse stops (always good information to have), and you can spend a few minutes asking for head and neck flexes, which also help you establish leadership.

In asking for the stop, determine if the horse responds to a voice cue, or if you also need to use seat, hands, and legs, or any combination thereof. This information is a big factor in rider safety and may come in very handy later on.

The flexes are similar to what was done during the ground assessment, but as responses often change when a horse is bearing weight, it is good to do these with a rider and note any differences from the unmounted response. To ask the horse to flex, steady the horse's body with your legs, then gently ask the horse to bring his nose to the left without any forward motion from his feet.

Remember that each horse you look at may have had a different method of training. Some may have been started with natural horsemanship, others with traditional dressage. There are many ways to ask a horse to bend, flex, turn, or perform any task you ask, so be patient and give the horse credit for trying, even if he does not respond with the intent the rider had in mind. Ideally, your prospective horse will be able to reach his nose back far enough on both sides to easily touch the toe of the rider's boot.

THE WALK

The rider from your team should be skilled enough to discern specific pelvic movement at the walk. This is important not only for any program participant who might ride the horse; it is also another way to assess the horse's soundness.

To assess movement, the rider should ask the horse for a good working walk, then sit in a balanced seat with a neutral pelvis, one that is not tilted forward or back. The rider can then feel whether the horse's movement rocks her pelvis and hips in a forward and back motion, one that is side to side, or a movement that combines the two into a figure eight rotational movement.

This mare shows a relaxed walk and has an ear focused on her rider.

The gait should also be evaluated at a slow walk and at a power walk. Many horses provide a different movement with a slower or faster walk. Your center or program should strive to have horses that provide a variety of rider pelvic movements at the walk. Maybe you already have a horse of similar size and temperament who provides good front to back rider pelvic movement, but this horse you are evaluating provides a gentler movement. This new horse could then be a fit for riders who are more physically fragile.

The rider should also feel the horse provide a continual, even movement with all four legs. A horse who walks one, two . . . THREE, four, could jar some riders who have a physical disability. In this way the horse would be limited as to the kind of rider he could benefit. A horse who walks in this manner could also have a stifle, hip, lower back, or hock issue that might limit the amount of weight he can carry.

As a rule of thumb, a center needs a big horse to carry big riders. If the large horse has weight restrictions due to soreness or arthritis, then he may not be as valuable to your program as you had hoped. This is particularly true in therapeutic vaulting where an even stride is especially important. A horse who provides an even one, two, three four movement is much preferred, although they are sometimes hard to find.

THE TROT

Depending on the needs of your program, the horse should have a slow, even trot. Besides the fact that a big trot throws many beginning and newly-independent riders off-balance, these horses can be hard to keep up with if your rider needs a sidewalker. On the plus side, however, a jolting trot teaches riders who are able, to keep their heels down and also helps riders who have trouble with attention (autism spectrum, ADD or ADHD) and focus.

THE CANTER

The canter and the lope are synonymous, just different terms used by English and western riders respectively. Technically, if performed to perfection, the lope will be a slower, flatter-strided version of the canter, which will have more impulsion. The foot falls are exactly the same and the difference is only in how the horse is ridden. For our purposes here, the term canter is used.

Not every horse at your center will need to canter in your program, obviously, but if the horse can canter while bearing weight, then the horse has a better chance of staying fit. Endurance riders know that trotting builds endurance and stamina, but cantering builds lung capacity. The canter also works different muscles than the trot, important muscles that are needed to maintain a strong back.

If you envision the horse as a help to your students who canter, or if you have advanced therapeutic vaulters, then a nice, easy canter and canter departure are necessary. The stride should be slow and performed with even rhythm, and the downward transition should be just as slow and easy as the transition upward. The horse should also be able to canter well on both leads.

Often, horses who are donated to centers are not able to canter safely with program participants. Some of this is due to temperament; the horses get too excited when a rider does not have a sufficient seat or good rein control. Other factors include breed, conformation, training and soreness. Drafty breeds are bred to pull and often have an awkward canter where the horse pulls more with his front end than he pushes from his hind. The result is an uncollected, unbalanced gait.

Horses who have high knee and hock action often bring this to their canter stride, which can provide too much motion for a rider who is just learning to canter. Oddly enough, the big sport horses, the ones who have the most bone-jarring trots, often have slow, smooth, rocking chair canters. If you and your rider can get past the horse's size, these horses also typically have excellent upward and downward gait transitions as they are bred and trained to canter and jump, rather than trot, as draft horses are.

Many horses have never been taught a good canter transition. Being able to canter from the walk is nice, as it eliminates the possibility of entering the canter from a fast trot, which results in a fast, ungainly, unbalanced canter. Whether or not you can teach an older horse a walk/canter transition depends on how deeply his original training is ingrained, and also his physical ability. If the horse is sore or arthritic, it could be physically difficult for the horse to perform a nice canter departure from the walk while weight bearing.

How important these things are to you depend on your original reasons for looking at the horse. What purpose will this particular horse serve in your program?

THE BACK

Many centers never ask their horses to back within the lesson. Backing is a riding skill, so those participants will have a gap in their education if that skill is not taught. However, if the herd at your center is older, and your veterinarian believes it is not a good activity for your herd, then a "no backing" policy is probably needed.

The back will tell you two main things: how easily the horse gives his head and whether or not the horse is sore. If the horse backs easily and straight, you are good to go, but that is rarely the case. Some horses refuse to back because they have not been asked recently and it is an issue of dominance. The horse will test in this area to see if the rider is deserving of the leadership needed to get him to back.

The most common reason for a refusal to back, though, is soreness. It hurts to have someone on his back, and then have to back up. One person should watch the horse's tail during the back to see if it remains flat, or if it moves to the left or right. Another should watch the ears and head position. Pinned ears, or a nose that is raised higher than the ears are a good indication that backing is probably not in this horse and rider's immediate future. In fact, if the rider presses on, then there is a good chance that the horse's next move will be a rear.

Normally if you ask a horse to do something, you want to see it through. But in this instance, you are there only to assess the horse, not give a training session. Safety comes first, so simply ask the horse to back and record whatever response is given.

ADVANCED MOVES

The ability to perform movements such as a sidepass, shoulder in, or a turn on the forehand or hindquarters, shows off both the horse's training and his physical ability. Some of these moves are considered lateral, where the horse moves sideways, or forward and sideways, at the same time. The use of the word lateral and exactly what it refers to is again determined by discipline. An advanced western rider will give a slightly different definition than an advanced English rider.

Any time a horse can cross one leg over the other while carrying a rider, he strengthens important muscles that will keep him going well into old age. These muscles are predominantly abdominal and leg muscles, and the advanced moves also free and strengthen the horse's shoulder and hip.

As with backing, many horses have never been taught advanced moves. And again, how much he can learn will depend on breed, conformation, training, and existing level of arthritis or soreness. The fact that the horse cannot perform any of these moves should not necessarily be a deterrent, unless you need a horse who can teach riders these moves. A red flag should pop up, though, if a horse can move one direction, but not the other. This is a sign of soreness, muscle atrophy, old injury, arthritis, or a combination of all of the above.

If your rider has the skill, she should ask the horse to halfpass (simultaneously move forward and sideways) at the walk. If successful, then ask at the trot, and at the canter. If the horse can perform these moves equally well both left and right he has a better chance of being productive at a center well into his twenties. One Arabian gelding who had fourth level dressage training was at a therapeutic riding center teaching advanced riders how to do a halfpass when he was twenty-five. With staff he could do flying lead changes every other stride and back a figure eight.

Many centers have a cut-off age for horses who come into the center. That age might be in the neighborhood of eighteen, as many centers hope to get at least five years of full service from every horse they bring in. There is a lot of time, training, and effort that goes into the making of a therapy horse and the longer the horse can be part of the program, the more time and effort that can be spent in other areas. There is always something to do at a therapeutic riding center!

However, if the horse is healthy and sound, good-natured and fits your needs, then an assessment of an older (or younger) horse might be a good idea. His age is just one more element to consider.

THE THERAPEUTIC MOUNT

Up until this point, every detail that has been assessed is something I would do for every horse I looked at, whether the horse is for a therapy program or an individual. It is now time to add therapeutic support people into the mix, such as leaders and sidewalkers, to see how the horse will react.

To do this, go back to the mount and simulate as closely as possibly the process of a typical therapeutic mount. You might also choose to have a different rider for these next portions of the assessment, as long as the rider meets the horse's weight requirements. It helps if the rider can play the role of a person with a specific disability, the type of rider with a disability who might actually ride the horse at your center.

How does the horse react when a leader, rider, and two sidewalkers crowd around him during the mount? Remember that this is probably a new experience for the horse, so you are evaluating the horse's sensibility and willingness to try, rather than his actual skill in this area. After he arrives on your property, you can teach him what he needs to know.

When the rider makes noise or walks with a limp, what is the horse's reaction? How about when the rider digs a toe into the horse's side during the mount, drags a foot over the horse's rump, or lands with her chest on the horse's neck. Remember to go slowly here. The idea is not to frighten the horse or push him so far outside his comfort zone that people get hurt. Instead, gently simulate these scenarios to see where his comfort level is.

LEADERS

With the exception of horses who compete in lead line classes at a show, most horses are not used to being led with a rider, so this may be another new experience. The horse's sensibility and willingness go a long way here, too, even if the horse is not sure what is expected of him.

With rider aboard, the leader should lead with little help from the rider at the walk and trot from the left side, and then again from the right. Also try turning, stopping, and backing. For safety purposes the horse's ear or eye should stay next to the leader's shoulder, as the leader needs to have a visual of the horse's eye and ear to quickly assess the horse's emotions and mood during the assessment.

Some horses who have been trained using natural horsemanship may be at a disadvantage, as they have been taught to follow their leader, rather than walk next to them. While this can be a good way to establish trust

This leader is in good position to see the horse's ears and facial expression, and also keep good control.

and leadership with your horse, imagine what might happen to a rider with cerebral palsy or developmental delay if the horse spooked at a scary object to his rear, scooted forward, and knocked his leader aside. Fortunately, most horses easily understand they are now being led in a different manner, and are happy to adjust.

The other extreme is the pushy horse who is too forward and continually tries to walk ahead of his leader. If the leader ends up back by the horse's chest or shoulder, much control is lost. This horse may always be a difficult lead, as "pushy" is part of his personality.

Finally there is the horse who begrudges any kind of forward movement at all. Confusion at being led at the same time a rider is on his back aside, these horses have usually been allowed to develop sloppy leading manners by their owners. With a firm set of new rules in place, most balky horses eventually do very well.

SIDEWALKERS

Sidewalkers provide important physical or cognitive support to the rider during the lesson, and one or two sidewalkers may walk close to the horse throughout the session. If there is only one sidewalker, he or she is usually on the off (or right) side. If a second sidewalker is needed, that person is on the left, behind the leader.

Some horses are uncomfortable when sidewalkers stand close to the horse and rider. Others are okay with one sidewalker, but not two.

Not every rider needs a sidewalker, and that's a good thing because many horses are uncomfortable with them. We've all encountered a person who stands too close to us in conversation and their closeness makes us feel uncomfortable. Just as people have a circle of personal space, so do horses, and sidewalkers continually invade a horse's space.

Besides unsoundness, the number one reason a horse is found not suitable for a therapy program is because he or she cannot tolerate sidewalkers. And, that is something that is rarely changed with training. Either a horse is comfortable with sidewalkers inside his space, or he isn't. Some horses will tolerate one sidewalker, but not two. On the other hand, I have participated in several lessons where an especially gifted horse has not minded three or four sidewalkers.

Some very calm and well-trained horses have huge circles of personal space, so be cautious when you first add a sidewalker to your assessment. Be sure to add the sidewalker while stopped. The sidewalker should walk on the right side of the horse close enough to do a thigh hold. This is when the sidewalker places the fingers of his or her left hand around the front of the saddle and drapes the left arm across the rider's thigh. Be sure the sidewalker does not dig an elbow into the horse's back. Other team members can take note of the horse's response. Did he pin his ears? Try to cow kick? Refuse to move?

If the horse is comfortable with the first sidewalker, a second one should come in on the left. For safety, be sure to stop the horse as each sidewalker is added. This second sidewalker will also do a thigh hold, but use his or her right hand and arm.

A few turns, stops, and periods of walking and trotting with the sidewalkers is all that is needed. The horse may be quite confused by this time, so be sure to score the try, rather than the result.

SENSITIVITY

Knowing how sensitive the horse is to aids and rider movement is also a key component of your assessment. To start, have your rider lean forward, back, left, and right. Then record the horse's response. Ideally, the horse should attempt to move underneath the rider when the rider, for example, leans her upper body to the left. This is a good sign that the horse is trying to take care of his mounted person. It also lets you know that the horse is aware of balance and is trying to balance himself and his rider.

Some horses stop when the rider begins to lean, and that is not an altogether bad response, either. It may interrupt the lesson, but everyone remains safe. Better that than the horse who scoots forward, which can be hard for the leader to control. This leaning simulates an unbalanced rider, one who could have cerebral palsy, development delay, injury, curvature of the spine, or a host of other disabilities.

Then ask the rider to touch the horse's ears and the top of his tail. Of course only ask if, based on the horse's previous responses, you and the rider feel comfortable with this activity. Try this at a standstill and while at the walk. A two point while being led at the walk and trot, arms to the side or above the rider, is another good test. Hope for the horse's awareness of these movements, but little response.

Next, the rider can try making noise, such as a quick shout, loud laugh, even clapping hands together. Many horses are uncomfortable with sounds they cannot see the source of, or with verbal sounds from a rider that the horse does not understand. Expect to see the horse swivel his ears toward the sound. With luck, he will also remain quiet.

Again, the goal here is not to frighten the horse, but to see what he is comfortable with and accepting of. All noise and movement should start slowly and softly, and gradually increase only to the point of what the horse might experience during a lesson. If the horse is unduly concerned before that point, though, stop and move on to something else.

Lastly, the rider should scissor her legs back and forth; left leg back while the right leg is forward. Back and forth several times to see how the horse responds. Do not worry if the horse rushes forward, but it is a good idea to be prepared for that response. If the horse is sensitive to leg pressure, this is often an easy redirect for the horse with some desensitizing and repeated scissoring.

These activities should give you a good assessment of the horse's sensitivity. You can also try riding backward, riding draped over the saddle with the rider's head on one side of the horse and both legs on the other, briefly and gently digging a heel or toe into the horse's side, wiggling in the saddle, or any other movement you feel is safe but necessary for you to get an honest assessment of the horse.

TOYS AND GAMES

Your center might not use a lot of toys and games in either your mounted or unmounted activities. However, it is always good to assess your prospective horse in this area, as the horse's response gives a good idea as to what his reaction might be if, say, a plastic bag blew across his path in an outdoor arena, or if a volunteer took off a windbreaker and placed it on the railing of your riding ring.

You have already done similar activities on the ground, but adding a rider can make a difference. For some horses, an unusual object, a rider, a leader, *and* a sidewalker can be too much, and understandably so. Other horses find themselves interested in the object and want to play, too!

If the horse did not score well with toys and games on the ground, consider skipping this part of the assessment with a rider aboard. But, if the horse was comfortable with the earlier use of toys, then a nerf toy or other small, soft, squishy object is a good place to start. Always take time to introduce an object to the horse by letting him smell it, then toss it along his neck, or drop it where he can see it. Then hand the toy to the rider and have the leader ask the horse to walk on.

Try a gentle game of catch with the rider and a sidewalker, always keeping in mind the horse's comfort level and reaction. If the horse is concerned, just stop. If not, the rider can throw the toy out and ahead of the horse at a ten o'clock or a two o'clock position, or just drop the toy as the team is walking.

Another easy object to bring along is a small bell. Bells can be used with visually impaired riders to cue a head turn, a stop, or any other action, especially if the rider does not respond to verbal instructions. Here, repeat the process of introduction, then show the horse that the new toy makes noise. But, instead of bouncing a hard object off the horse, the sidewalker can slowly ring the bell near the rider's hand or knee. If the horse is okay with the movement and the noise, hand the bell to the rider, who can slowly ring it from several positions above the horse. Over the neck, wither, hip, and near the rider's head are a few suggestions.

A small ball the rider can toss to roll along the ground, several large rings the rider can rattle or beat together to make noise, or other object you regularly use in activities at your center can also be tested. Even if you do very little mounted work at your center, if you offer driving or ground activities, it is good to know as much as you can about this horse before you make a decision, and these exercises allow you to do that.

Keep in mind the needs of your program five years in the future. How will this horse fit into that vision? Could he also be a vaulting horse? A horse you take to community events to spread awareness of your program? A horse who teaches students in a ground program how to longe a horse?

THE HALT

As riders, trainers, and instructors, we spend so much time asking our horses to move forward that we often forget to teach our equine partners that it is okay to be still for long periods of time. Before you dismount is a good time to assess how well the horse stands still with a rider on his back.

Consider all the time it can take during a therapeutic lesson to adjust the rider's stirrups, position the rider, tighten the girth, make sure the saddle is centered on the horse's back, give special encouragement, explain a concept thoroughly, or give a lesson summary. Much of this is done with the horse and rider at the halt.

Even though you have worked with the horse for a while now, there is still much to learn at the halt. What is the horse's attitude now, as compared to the beginning of the assessment? Is the horse calm? Fidgety? Cranky? Or, did he close his eyes for a quick nap? While calm is nice, it is not unheard of for a horse to fall asleep during a lesson and either buckle at the knee or go down altogether.

This is also a good time to tell the horse what a fine being he is. Praise should have been given throughout, but now you can lavish great admiration onto him. For better or worse, the horse gave you what he had, and that should be acknowledged.

DISMOUNT

As with the mount, the dismount should be an approximation of an average dismount at your center. Just safely recreate that environment here. If the horse seems calm, you might try an over the crest dismount, where the rider's right leg swings over the horse's neck, rather than the horse's croup, or a dismount to the right side of the horse. By now you should have a good idea of what the horse will and will not tolerate. Think it through, discuss with your team, then execute it, keeping the horse's body language foremost in your mind.

HIPPOTHERAPY, VAULTING, AND DRIVING

Many of the activities we have discussed have involved therapeutic riding or ground programs. If the horse you are looking at will be involved in hippotherapy, driving, or vaulting, of course you must evaluate the horse in those areas, too.

HIPPOTHERAPY

The horse's movement and gait are so critical to the success of a hippotherapy session that you will want, if at all possible, your therapist to be part of your team that visits the horse. Then the therapist can sit on the horse to see if the movement is what he or she needs.

If your therapist cannot visit with you, then the assessments that involve movement and gait should be as detailed as possible. A video of the horse at the walk and trot can also be helpful for the therapist to view later.

Sometimes horses in hippotherapy are led, and other times they are driven from the ground. If you drive your hippotherapy horses even some of the time, this skill should be evaluated, too. The owner might not have driving lines, so be sure to bring some of those along, as well as a surcingle, pad, and any other equipment you might use during a normal session.

If the horse has never before been driven from the ground, know that this is an easy skill to teach most horses, as driving works off the horse's natural herd instinct and behavior. When a lead mare wants to move a subordinate member of the herd, she moves that horse from behind, and so it is with driving. The driver drives the horse forward from behind.

Mounted evaluations should include all of the assessments just mentioned, and also a short mock hippotherapy session. In hippotherapy, a physical or occupational therapist often places the rider in seemingly odd positions on the horse and incorporates the movement of the horse to benefit the rider's physical condition. Some of these movements might include the rider lying backward on the horse, which puts the rider's head near the top of the horse's tail, riding sideways, or leaning forward on the horse's neck.

If the rider and the rest of your team feel it is safe to do so, a few of these positions should be tried and the horse's response noted. As long as the horse is calm and willing, much of what is needed from the horse can be taught once he is at your center—with the exception of gait and movement. There, the horse either has it or he doesn't.

DRIVING

Therapeutic driving horses need a lot of documented hours in front of a cart before they can be incorporated into a lesson. If the horse you are looking at has been driven for some time, and the hours have been recorded and verified, you may be able to get him into your program within several months. If not, it may be several years. But, if the horse is a good prospect, he may be worth the wait, especially if he can be involved in other lessons in the meantime.

Evaluate the horse's driving ability from the ground if no cart or buggy is available, or if you are unsure of the safety of hitching up the horse.

As with hippotherapy, bring as much driving equipment with you as you can, with the exception of a cart. If the horse is not currently a solid driving horse, do not try to hook him up for the assessment. Instead just evaluate his education, or lack of, in ground driving. If he is a seasoned driving horse, the owner will probably have a cart to use and a harness that fits.

While it is important to observe all possible safety precautions during the entire evaluation, it is even more important here. If the horse is being hitched, double check all of the owner's equipment and work, and as with riding, be sure the owner drives first.

When a member of your team drives, be sure to assess all stop and go transitions, turns and backing, as well as circles. The quiet stand still is important, too. Then ask the horse to drive while being led. This could be another odd request for a horse to process, so be prepared for a little confusion. Also, how is the horse to work with on the ground? Many driving programs include lessons on the harness and harnessing, so a patient, well-mannered, seasoned driving horse with good ground manners is another great find.

But, just as all under saddle horses are not suitable for therapeutic riding programs, not all driving horses make good therapeutic driving horses. The horse might have too much pep, or need a very firm hand to maintain control. Or, the horse could be too lazy, and take too much effort to reach effective forward motion. Your team knows the needs of your program, and whether or not this horse is a good candidate.

VAULTING

Therapeutic vaulting typically involves a lot of physical activity from a group of people around the horse as part of the lesson. While one or two vaulters are on the horse, the other vaulters might walk safely behind or next to the horse in step with the horse's stride, run around the outside of the circle the horse is being longed in, play catch with a large (or small) ball, or move into the same positions on a series of barrels placed around the outside of the longeing circle as the vaulter(s) on the horse.

Vaulting is done with a special vaulting surcingle that the current owner of the horse may not have, so be sure to bring one along, along with a vaulting headstall, side reins, longe line and vaulting whip. One of your team members can perform basic vaulting moves as part of this specific evaluation. Evenness of stride and gait are very important here, as is smoothness. Most vaulting horses have wide backs, which makes it easier for the vaulter to perform the various vaulting moves.

Vaulting horses need lots of hours of being longed before he or she can be an effective lesson partner. These horses also often carry more than one vaulter, and are sized accordingly. If your team collectively feels that it is safe to put two people up onto the horse, the process will give you a good idea how suited the horse is for this activity.

Specific feedback to look for from the horse includes how well the horse longes. Does he tolerate the side reins well? Does activity outside the longeing circle distract the horse? How smooth are the horse's upward and downward gait transitions? Does the horse move forward willingly? Will the horse stop and stand for several minutes at a time?

However you hope the horse will fit into your program, by now you should have a very good idea of the potential of this horse. But, there are a few things left to find out before you make a final decision.

History 14

After you are done with the evaluation, you have enough knowledge to ask the owner more detailed questions about the horse. Basic information will have been provided in the horse donation profile, and someone from your committee will have spoken with the owner over the phone before your visit, but until you have seen and worked with the horse, you may not know enough to ask the right questions.

We are all a product of our environment and a horse is no different. An early injury, a barn fire, or a previous job pulling a hay wagon might not be on the horse's donation profile. However, during the assessment you might have seen evidence of the fire or injury, or suspected that the horse was far more experienced than the owner had indicated.

Information about the horse's likes and dislikes might also come to light. Did the horse not like the plastic bag? The owner might have a story about that, and that information could give you insight as to whether the fear is deep seated or superficial. Deep fears are tough to overcome, whether by horse or human. Superficial fears are typically not severe, and through desensitizing or a new set of kind but firm rules, the fears can be replaced with good thoughts and behavior.

A few years ago I worked with a former pony horse. This horse had escorted racehorses onto the track for many years. He did not bat an eye at cheering crowds, flags, pennants, banners, loudspeakers, or nervous horses, but came completely undone at the sight of a white plastic grocery bag. It was also discovered that the mere thought of his rider opening a mailbox sent him into a dizzying spin, and a T-bar with rings on the other side of the arena? No way.

When the horse first came to the therapy program the center had not done a full evaluation. Sound, retired pony horse? They said to bring him on over. While he was an excellent walk/trot horse for independent riders and did not mind being led while two sidewalkers assisted a physically fragile rider, if a toy or game was mistakenly left out in the arena, he became unsafe. Finally the center called the donor, who called the horse's former owner and it turned out that before his job ponying racehorses, the horse had been in a mild trailer accident.

On his way to a trail ride competition, the horse's then owner had trail obstacles in the adjacent trailer stall, and a white rain slicker and a large inflated ball landed on the horse during the accident. The horse was not hurt physically, but obviously was emotionally scarred. Even though the horse was very good at what he did at the center, staff there felt it was in his best interests not to try to get him past his long-standing fears, and instead his donor turned him out into a field with several retired race horses for a much-deserved rest.

Hopefully the horse you look at will not have had such a traumatic experience, but questions such as "How did he get this scar?" or "How long has he pinned his ears when he goes into a trot?" will deepen the horse's story. If the owner says this is the first time the horse has pinned his ears (and you believe her), then he may just be overwhelmed by the assessment process and think he'd rather be back in his pasture. If this is an ongoing thing for him it may just be habit, or it may be soreness.

If you know more of the horse's history it allows you to put a context to the information you learned during the assessment. Was the pony lazy? How long has he been ridden by little children? Maybe he just needs some new rules. Or, he could have arthritis.

This is your opportunity to ask the owner anything you have a question about. If the horse scored low on how far he was able to flex but did flex evenly, for example, knowing that this seventeen-year-old horse has been turned out in the pasture for the past two years gives some hope that with regular work he may become more flexible. When all is said and done the assessment is a tool to help you make an informed decision. Based on the horse's history, you may choose to take the stiff, willing horse over the perfectly sound and flexible horse who has a pushy personality. It all goes back to the needs of your center. Which horse is going to be the most versatile, or best fit a specific population of program participants?

The next step is to decide whether or not you want to bring the horse to your center for a ninety-day trial. Your entire committee, including those who were not able to be there for the assessment, should make that decision. So, before you leave, give the owner a time frame for your answer. Ideally, your equine committee should meet within a few days, but if you have several horses to look at and compare, it might be two weeks. Whatever the time frame though, stick to whatever you tell the owner.

Only rarely should you give an owner an answer at the end of the assessment. People tend to get excited about the possibility of a new horse, but are more realistic after they have had a night to sleep on the decision. Plus, you may have other, more suitable, horses to see.

If the horse is lame or if you did not complete the assessment for another reason, you may choose to keep the door open. "We saw some possibilities. When the problem is fixed (or the weather improves, or the horse's feet have been trimmed) let us know and if the slot we have available in our herd is still open, we'll come back."

Words like these also allow you to close the door to this horse without offending the owner. These words imply it is not the horse who is not suitable, but that there is no longer an opening. Owners never want to be told their horses are deficient. We'll talk more about that in Chapter 18.

Mares or Geldings? 15

For most centers it doesn't matter what sex the prospective horse is. It should go without saying that a stallion is not appropriate, but there are some things to think about when considering either a mare or a gelding.

THE BEAUTY OF MARES

While mares can be wonderful, most people know they come into season roughly very three weeks. Some mares show no behavioral changes during this time, while others become so distracted that it is difficult to get them to focus. Your mare may stamp or squeal when either horses or people come near, or she might become frantic when separated from her best friend. She might swish her tail or try to nip. Under saddle she could whinny and dance, hump her back or kick when leg pressure is applied, or completely ignore her leader or rider.

Depending on what you need your horse to do, "mareish" behavior could be a red flag. On the other hand, depending on the type of participant and the kind of service(s) you offer, a mare who is distracted when in heat can serve as a great spring board for discussing focus, impulsive behavior, health, and depending on the participant, even the facts of life.

Some mares become quite moody when they come into heat and if the moodiness extends to crankiness, she may need to sit out of lessons for a few days. This brings up the ongoing problem of repeatedly having to substitute another horse into the lesson, and if the horse/human bond is important to participants who interact with this mare, it can slow their progress.

If a mare acts as if she is always in heat, then the problem might be more than just hormones. She could be dealing with soreness, dental problems, or even an ovarian cyst or tumor, so more than the usual pre-donation vet check may be required.

If her heat cycle is the only negative, and she is otherwise fabulous for your center, there are options. You can regulate the cycle and diminish the behavior issues with hormones or bio-identical hormones. Cost has to be a consideration, as does the practicality of administering the treatments. Do you have the staff or volunteers in place to ensure the hormones are given when they should be, and can your center afford them? Or, you could try light massage or soothing music before her lesson.

Another problem is that you may not know how she will respond until you have the mare on your property during a strong spring or fall heat cycle. While mareish behavior should be noted on your horse donation profile, it isn't always. Many owners want so badly to either donate the horse, or unload a liability, that they aren't always truthful when they fill out the form. That's why it's great if one of your staff or volunteers knows the donor or the horse, though that is not always possible.

With all that to consider, mares can be very loving toward program participants. In the wild they are the nurturers, and without a foal to take care of, a mare will often take better care of her riders than a gelding will. I once witnessed a developing bond between an ancient Arabian mare and a young boy with cerebral palsy. The boy was nonverbal when he first began riding, but after weeks and weeks of his wheelchair being rolled up to the mare, and the mare voluntarily dropping her face into his lap so he could hug her, one day during this process the boy simply said "Hi."

It was the first word that young man had ever spoken and his instructor, leaders, and sidewalkers all had to take a moment to shed tears before they could proceed with that day's activities. Since then the boy has gained enough verbal skill to tell his parents his wants and needs with one-word directives, statements, and answers. Without the kind nurturing of that old mare, he may never have progressed that far.

When I was showing horses I always told the owners of the horses in my stable that geldings were consistent, steady, and reliable in competition, and mares could be across the board in their performance. But, when a mare was "on," she was brilliant. I still feel that way, no matter what the job or activity. That's just one reason I am a little sad when I come across a center that only has geldings.

I understand the thought process behind the practice. No mares on property means no horses have to deal with heat cycles. No gelding is distracted by a mare who is in season, and no horses have to be substituted when a mare is so silly that she doesn't need to be in lessons that day. But in addition to losing those moments of brilliance that only a mare can bring, there is the herd dynamic to consider.

THE IMPORTANCE OF A BALANCED HERD

I encourage providers of equine therapy to keep their horses in as natural a state as possible. This includes a herd-like atmosphere. Unfortunately, many centers have little in the way of pasture or turnout. But if staff members at these programs are creative, they can still foster a herd environment and the all-important herd dynamic.

A natural herd, of course, typically includes a stallion, a small number of mares, and a lot of young horses. Each member of the herd has his or her place and a job. We have to remember that even though our horses are part of our team, they are not human team members. Our horses still think, see, hear, smell, taste, and move like the equines they are. If our horses are to be the best team members they can be, we need to offer the closest thing we can to their natural state and (in an ideal world) that is a mixed herd.

Those who watch and study domestic horses have long known that herds made up solely of geldings can become sleep deprived. As you might imagine, horses who fail to sleep enough do not feel safe. If the herd does not have a dominant mare, the hierarchy in the herd is disrupted, and the geldings do not feel safe enough to lie down and stretch out flat to achieve the deep sleep that they need.

In the wild, the alpha mare's duty is to tend to the safety of the herd; this is essential to their survival. It is the alpha mare's job to signal the herd to move, sleep, eat, drink, or run for safety. It has been found that, on average, geldings make poor leaders and provide inadequate herd safety.

Joe Bertone, DVM, MS, DACVIM, confirmed this in an *EQUUS* article in February 2007. In the article, he mentioned studies that show that horses look to the nearest mare before they lie down. Horses feel safer knowing a mare is on lookout duty. Equine society is quite matriarchal, and while geldings can fill this role it is better if it is done by a mare.

Many programs I see have both mares and geldings, but keep them in separate pastures to lessen the attraction, and distraction. It is a solution, especially if the fields adjoin and the boys and girls can see each other. I have actually witnessed one lead mare control several small herds in different pastures because they could see her.

Programs with little turnout can try a mixed herd turn out at regular times in their arena. A mixed herd of the same four or five turned out together for an hour a day (or even every other day) helps our therapy partners be better horses.

AGE

Age is an offshoot of the mare/gelding dilemma. Just like human families, wild horse herds have members of all age ranges. This is important because younger horses learn from older ones, especially older mares. In this way, a newer member of a therapeutic herd who is ten or twelve learns the ropes from the twenty-two-year-old.

Many centers have a policy that when a horse is too old to be ridden or driven, they are retired and found a nice home. This is due to the economics of the program, especially if it is a nonprofit. There is only so much money and it needs to be spent on horses who provide the bulk of the services. Plus, as the herd ages, it does not make sense to have a lot of older horses.

But what economists, bookkeepers, accountants, and board members often do not realize is that an older horse is a stabilizing influence on the herd. An older mare is much like a grandmother. Her wisdom is trusted, and her common sense trickles down to the other horses. To much the same extent, it is the same with an older gelding. These senior horses can also still teach participants about grooming, health care, parts of the horse, stable management, and much more.

The question then not only is: mare or gelding; it becomes: older mare/older gelding?

THE FINAL TALLY

When it comes to a gelding, he can be a wonderfully consistent, reliable, steady therapy partner for participants. A mare can be loving, nurturing and intuitive, but unfocused when in heat. The important thing is to offer the most balanced herd possible, one that also that meets the needs of your program, your horses, and your participants.

Every program is different, with unique facility set-ups and participant needs. Your team knows what is best for your center and how your staff and volunteers can best manage your herd. Both mares and geldings can be outstanding in the field of equine therapy, and the sex of your prospective therapy horse is just one of many considerations.

PART III

Donation, Lease, or Purchase? 16

Some horses are donated to therapeutic centers, some are leased, and a few are even purchased. Which scenario happens for which horse depends on your budget, your center's guidelines, and your relationship with the owner. There are pros and cons for all three.

DONATION

Many centers prefer to have the horse donated with the owner/donor having first right of refusal if and when the horse is retired from the center. This arrangement keeps the owner from expressing his or her thoughts about training, lesson assignments, veterinary care, turn-out, and other important decisions about the horse's health and well-being. That's an issue that pops up from time to time with a lease.

Most horse owners who are ready to let go of a particular horse have no problem with a donation. The owner/donor might be heading off to school, downsizing, or not able to care for a horse who no longer fits his or her needs. The fact is, most horses are treated exceedingly well at a therapeutic riding center and a donation is often a good option for all involved.

Some donors might have interest in a tax deduction, and depending on a number of variables, the donor may or may not be able to take one. The IRS requires a center to keep the horse in the program for a period of time before the donor can claim the deduction. If the horse is given back to the owner, another person, or sold before that time period is up, the deduction cannot be claimed.

Also, the center should not put a value on the horse for the donor's tax purposes. That is the job of the owner, or an independent equine appraiser whose expense should be covered by the donor. In one instance, a woman donated a high-profile horse who had developed ringbone. The horse, who was fifteen, could no longer perform the job she had been purchased for two years previously—for many tens of thousands of dollars. The prospective donor, wanting to cut her losses, called her local center to inquire about donating the horse. It turned out that the horse was a very good fit at the center, and the low level work did not bother the horse's arthritis.

The donor asked the center to sign a paper that stated the value of the horse as being what she had paid for it, but staff there wisely suggested she call an independent appraiser instead. An appraiser can only value the horse in her present condition and the addition of the ringbone, plus the fact that the horse had been out of competition for six months and was unlikely ever to return, greatly diminished her value. The horse stayed in the program much longer than the IRS's waiting period, but the donor could only claim a fraction of what she paid.

In a donation, the center usually has a ninety-day grace period from the day the horse first steps foot on center property until the donation is finalized. This ninety-day period is to allow for vet and farrier checks, and for the advanced training a horse needs to become a therapy horse. Sometimes a horse will excel during an assessment, but during the ninety-day trial staff finds that the horse is just not a good fit for a program. This is especially true if the horse has lived most of his life in the owner's backyard.

A horse who has been turned out to pasture, or who has lived in quiet surroundings and then goes to a program, is similar to a person who has been marooned for a time on a desert island and is then dropped into the heart of New York City. At many centers there is a lot going on, especially during lesson hours. It might be too much for a horse who is used to calmer and quieter conditions.

In addition, the horse might not pass a vet or farrier check, or be uncomfortable with wheelchairs and a mounting ramp. The horse might also not get along in the herd or be hard to catch. The reasons a horse might not stay for the full ninety-day trial period are too numerous to mention, but the donor needs to understand that while the horse is at your center, your staff will make feed, heath care, and training decisions for the horse, just as you would if the donation was final.

LEASE

A lease often works well if the horse will be at the center for a short time. Let's say two of your three big horses will be out of lessons for various reasons for the next sixty to ninety days. An abscess or strained tendon might be a cause. A friend, volunteer, board member, or another person familiar with your program has offered to lease the center his draft cross until one of the other two horses are back in the program. The horse is a former schooling horse and several instructors are familiar with her.

This scenario can work, as long as your team still does a full assessment (so you can familiarize yourself with as many details as possible about the horse). This assessment might be done on center grounds after the horse has arrived, but it should be done all the same. You never want to put a horse or a program participant into an unknown situation.

Even though the horse is needed in lessons today, be sure to take several weeks to familiarize the horse with her expected duties, and to arrange several pretend lessons to give the horse some experience. As a rule, most horses need a ninety-day period of acclimation, evaluation, and training before going into an actual lesson. Others show a lot of promise after ninety days but need even more time.

This kind of temporary solution can sometimes be beneficial. You must be absolutely sure, however, that the horse is ready to go into lessons before you actually place her into one. Program participants, their families, and insurance companies have a huge trust that centers have adequately prepared each horse in the program.

Other times a lease might be considered is when an owner is not ready to fully let go of the horse. The owner might want riding privileges, or a say in the horse's care. These situations often do not work out for the best. Donations or leases "with strings attached" need to be looked at carefully. Sometimes two well-intended parties start out with a vision of how the lease will work, but when placed into actuality, it becomes clear that the visions are miles apart. It becomes more difficult when the proposed lease is with the center and a board member or major donor, or with the center and an instructor or volunteer.

In the truest sense of a lease, the horse would go to a center and be treated as a donated horse for a specified time period. The arrangement becomes tricky when it is time for the horse to go home. If the horse is doing well, some people at the center might become upset if instructors want to keep the horse. The owner might be upset, too, for different reasons. She might not like the way the horse is shod, or the amount of weight the horse is carrying. Owners also have a hard time realizing that their seventeen-year-old horse is now twenty, and is not as strong or vibrant as she once was, even though the center gave her great care.

Another consideration is that your program put a lot of time and effort into training the horse. If the horse is good at her job and would normally stay if she had been donated, then additional staff time and/or volunteer hours are spent seeking out a replacement, having him or her vetted, and going through a training process. Or, the lease could be written so that the horse stays until the center feels it is time for the horse to retire from the program.

Without saying a lease is not a good idea, know that it is good to look at all the angles and include them in a written agreement. Some leases do turn out very well, and work for all concerned parties for many years.

PURCHASE

Most centers do not have funds to buy horses, but sometimes a grant or a cash donation specifically for the purchase of a horse is received. Being able to purchase a horse often allows a center to bring in a horse of a higher caliber then they might find otherwise.

The downside is that when most people sell a horse, they want it to stay sold. Most sellers are not comfortable with the idea of a ninety-day trial. Even if the horse passes the veterinary and farrier exams it is a huge risk of center funds to take on a horse who cannot be sent back if she does not work out.

Sometimes, however, the seller understands the process and is comfortable with the trial. The only risk then is that the owner is happy with the health, condition, and demeanor of the horse if it is, indeed, sent home.

One program that I worked with purchased a horse, then sixty days later sent him back. The horse was so uncomfortable with even one sidewalker that he cow kicked several members of the center staff who worked with her. When the horse came in, he was easily more than a hundred pounds overweight.

Under their veterinarian's care, they put the horse on a diet and exercise program and when he was sent home, he was much fitter than when he arrived. The owner, however, thought the horse was too thin (even though no one could see even one rib on the horse). She complained and made such a stink about her unhappiness that she mentioned it to everyone she saw. The result was that the center, through no fault of their own, lost a huge chunk of their stellar reputation. What followed was a loss of donations to the point that they had to scale back and regroup.

Donation, lease, or purchase, whichever option you choose, let the horse owner know up front what your center policies are with regard to the arrangement. Often, the only concern is that the owner gets the horse back when his or her time at your program is up. That is easily addressed in the agreement with a clause that gives the owner/donor first right of refusal when the horse is ready to retire.

Vet and Farrier Exams 17

Possibly the most overlooked parts of the entire horse selection process, whether for an individual, a stable, or a therapeutic riding center, are the vet and farrier (or trimmer) exams. Both of these give critical pieces of information and should answer any lingering questions you might have about the horse.

Usually, these exams are done after the horse is on center property. This means your team has met, assessed all of the information, and decided to give the horse a ninety-day trial. Any paperwork with the owner or donor should have been completed before the horse was picked up or delivered, or during that process.

Both the vet and farrier exams should be done as soon after the horse arrives as is convenient. After all, if it is determined that the horse is ouchy not due to a bad trim, but because he has Navicular disease, your team will have to make a tough decision that will probably send the horse back home.

So many hours go into getting a therapy horse ready to be in lessons that it is not productive to spend a lot of time on a horse, and then have him go right back to his owner due to poor health. In addition, staff and volunteers alike can quickly fall in love with a new arrival, so it is best to get the health and medical visits checked off and out of the way.

Many people do have a horse vet checked, but fewer call their farrier or trimmer in for a consultation. While a veterinarian is certainly qualified to treat a hoof and spot any red flags, a trimmer or farrier can possibly spot problems your veterinarian did not look for. During the vet exam, general health and soundness are the main things he or she will look for: teeth, hearing, vision, a full lameness check, and that ugly spot of dermatitis. If there are concerns, the veterinarian might suggest some x-rays to check for coffin bone rotation, or a scope to check for ulcers. Coffin bone rotation is an indication of founder or laminitis. Many owners do not even know that this has happened to their horse. Others do, but hope you won't notice.

The farrier, on the other hand, will look at the sole of the horse's hoof and tell you if the horse might be prone to stone bruising, or abscesses. She will tell you if the hoof wall is too damaged to hold a shoe, or if the horse is already shod, if the shoes are corrective, and why.

Shoeing is more costly than having a horse go barefoot, so ask your farrier or trimmer if this horse is a good barefoot candidate. Even if your center has hoof care services donated, someone is paying for the cost of the shoes and nails.

More people today than in even the recent past agree that it is better for a horse to go barefoot if at all possible, but not all can. Sometimes a horse who is barefoot has trouble because of the rough terrain or hard footing that surrounds a center. If you have a lot of gravel or rock, then more of your horses might have to wear shoes. One center tried for a year and a half to get a horse comfortable barefoot, but an old injury that distorted the shape of the hoof and the sole made that impossible. The horse now wears a nice set of front shoes about nine months out of the year, and does just fine.

As with the assessment, the recommendations you receive from your veterinarian and farrier or trimmer should be added to the overall picture of the horse. The information then, as a whole, can be used to make that final decision as to whether the horse goes home, or stays for her full ninety-day trial.

Yes, or No? 18

There are two situations where you will have to tell a horse owner yes or no. The first is within a few weeks of your team's assessment. You may have looked at several horses to fill a single available slot in your herd and that can take a little bit of time. The second is during the ninety-day trial period, when you make a final decision: to keep the horse or send her home.

If you have decided to give the horse a ninety-day trial, a simple email or phone call to the owner with the good news is in order. Then all you have to do is prepare the purchase, lease, or donation agreement, and make arrangements to pick up the horse or have him delivered.

If, however, your team decides after the assessment that the horse is not a good fit, it is courteous to tell the owner as soon as you make that decision. Most owners are disappointed, and understandably so. They saw your center as a loving place for their horse, and felt their baby would be well-cared for. Some owners may be facing a cash crunch and will be hard pressed to pay another month's board bill or for another shoeing. It could be the owner is moving and needs to place the horse quickly.

Other owners, however, do not understand why anyone would turn down their perfectly good horse. If the owner witnessed the assessment, the process hopefully was a good education for them. If he or she watched carefully, then they learned much about what their horse would be asked to do. Still, some owners are both upset and disappointed.

Without sharing the results of the entire assessment, you could say to the owner, "Your Walking Horse has a lovely walk, but we feel it is too fast for our sidewalkers to keep up with and that is a safety issue for us. Also, right now we need a horse who is shorter. I know you thought she was 14.3, but when we measured, she was 15.2. Thank you for showing her to us, though. If our needs change, we'll be back in touch. Maybe you will still have her." If you really did like the horse but she did not fit your needs, you could refer the owner to another program.

If you said yes after the assessment and brought the horse on property, and if the horse passed both the vet and farrier exam, at some point during the ninety-day trial period you will have all the information you need to make a final decision. You might find out two weeks in that the horse has a tendency to rear when he gets confused. Maybe he is a bully in the pasture, or rushes at other horses when they pass him in a lesson.

Those behaviors should cause some serious concerns. All are possibly "fixable" with a strong one-on-one horse/human relationship, but at a center, a horse might be handled by many people a day. Some of those people will not have great horse handling skills and a horse who already shows bad behavior can worsen under those conditions.

In a situation like this, the negative behavior should be well documented. Your center should already be documenting good and bad behavior from members of your herd, but every challenge and success of a horse who is on trial should be noted. Then, when a staffer has to call the owner, he or she has many strong, concrete reasons the horse is not a good fit.

Owners are often disappointed when a horse is sent home, and it can take a delicate balance of words and specifics to soothe an unhappy owner. "Scooter has not settled in well with our herd and has bitten two of our volunteers when they were leading him to the barn. He has also bucked twice when asked to trot during mock lessons, so we think he is not happy here. He does not want to be a therapy horse."

Most owners want what is best for their horse and the fact is: not every horse is cut out to be a therapy horse. It takes special physical, personality, and emotional gifts for a horse to excel in this field. That the horse did not pass the trial should not be held against the horse, it just was not a good fit. Some people are accountants and others are musicians. Some horses are jumpers; others excel on the trail. A special few are therapy horses.

My goal in writing this book was to give ideas for a detailed process in the selection of horses for both therapy and other purposes. You will, most likely, add some items to your assessment form and delete others. You will find your own processes, but the end result will be the same: a better fit for all concerned.

People often get carried away at the idea of a new horse and the assessment takes at least some of the emotion out of your choice. No one is happy when a horse does not work out. If a thorough, educated choice is made, however, you have a better chance of finding a good, long-term equine partner, no matter what you plan to do together.

In the field of equine assisted learning and therapy it takes time to train a horse to accept, for example, being led by a person in a wheelchair, standing still while a rider tries to toss a ball through a basketball net, unbalanced riders, or a person on the ground who might be having a meltdown. That training costs each center many staff and volunteer hours, plus the cost of the care of the horse. If you choose wisely, and get a horse who can benefit your program for five years or more, you have won the lottery.

Here's to you, and to all past, current, and future therapy horses. May you make a difference, learn about yourself and about life, meet great friends (both horse and human), and have some fun along the way. I invite you to learn more on my website at lisawysocky.com. Happy horse hunting!

Acknowledgements

It takes a village to create a book and I'd like to thank everyone who had a part in bringing *Therapy Horse Selection: A My Horse, My Partner Book* to you. Quincy and Tessie, two horses who are perfect in their imperfection, posed for most of the photographs. Quincy is a 16 hand, dark bay, solid colored Appaloosa gelding; and Tessie is a 15.2 hand, chestnut Belgian/Quarter Horse mare.

Letha Botts always has my back and her horses Gunner and Baby also participated in the photos. Gunner is a 15.2 hand, bay Tennessee Walking Horse; and Baby is a talkative 14.2 hand, black Walking Horse cross who prefers not to give out her age. To Kim Coleman Light and Kylan Jenkins who helped groom horses for the photos and helped with many of the shots, your contributions are invaluable. Thank you.

To all the wonderful people (and horses) at Central Kentucky Riding for Hope in Lexington, Kentucky, thanks for allowing me to use the photo of Dave, T-ball, and me during the World Equestrian Games (WEG) presentation on the cover. Fjords are so photogenic! Letha Botts, Carmen Lorentz, and Baby also nicely grace the cover and several interior pages. I also appreciate the use of the interior photo of Sampson, who lives at Shangri-La Therapeutic Academy of Riding in Lenoir City, Tennessee; and Spirit, who helps people in the Reinbow Riders program at the Tri-State Therapeutic Riding Center in Cleveland, Tennessee. Thank you all!

And to you, the reader: Thanks for your interest in therapy horses, and in the field of equine therapy in general. We may never know the huge impact these special horses have on others—and on ourselves.

When I started this book I had so much information to share that I was not sure how to include it all. One thought about gait, for instance, led me to the history of breeding Tennessee Walking Horses and from there to the geographic differences in PATH centers in Tennessee versus programs located in colder areas. My enthusiasm was so great that I had to rein myself in. The result is, hopefully, only information that involves horse selection. The rest will have to wait for another day—and another book.

From conformation to training, personality, and that special horse/human connection, many books have been written about each of those (and many other) aspects of horse selection. I hope you will consider this book as a jumping off point to learn more about specific items of interest to you. The future is now, and you *can* make a difference.

Appendix A: Equine Committee Application

For a downloadable copy of this form, please go to:
lisawysocky.com/therapyhorseselectionforms

Therapy Horse Selection: Equine Committee Application

Name: ______________________ Email address: ______________________

Address: ______________________

Home Phone: ______________________ Cell Phone: ______________________

How long have you been part of our center? ______________________

What initially led you to us? ______________________

In what capacities have you been involved here? ______________________

How long have you been involved with horses? ________ How many years have you ridden? ______

Please rate your horse experience on a scale of 1 (beginner) to 5 (expert): _________

Do you have a college degree in horse science or horse management? ❑ Y ❑ N

If yes, please describe: ______________________

Please list the equine activities you participate, or have participated, in (if any):

❑ Breeding # years_____ ❑ Driving # years_____ ❑ Eventing # years_____ ❑ FFA # years___

❑ 4-H # years_____ ❑ Instructing # years_____ ❑ Jumping # years_____ ❑ Polo # years___

❑ Ranch Sports # years_____ ❑ Showing # years_____ ❑ Trail Riding # years_____

❑ Training # years_____ ❑ Vaulting # years_____ ❑ Other ______________ # years___

Do you have any instructor certifications? ❑ PATH ❑ CHA ❑ ARIA ❑ Other ______________

Please list additional certifications (ESMHL, Advanced, Level III, etc.) ______________________

____

Do you ride: ❑ English ❑ Western ❑ Both ❑ Neither

What are your equine related strengths? ______________________

____

How could you best be an asset to our committee? ______________________

____

Why do you want to be part of the committee? ______________________

____

What else can you tell us about yourself? ______________________

____

OFFICE USE: Date Application Received:_________ Staff/Equine Committee Review: ____

Accepted? ❑ Y ❑ N Date applicant notified Y or N: _______

Appendix B: Program Participant Statistics

For a downloadable copy of this form, please go to:
lisawysocky.com/therapyhorseselectionforms

Therapy Horse Selection: Program Participant Statistics

Number of participants who are:
Male:
Female:
Total

Number of participants who are ages:
2 to 6:
7 to 10:
11 to 13:
14 to 18:
19 to 29:
30 to 39:
40 to 49:
50 to 59:
60 to 69:
70 to 79:
80+:

Number of participants who weigh:
Under 50 lbs.:
51-80 lbs.:
81-100 lbs.:
101-120 lbs.:
121-140 lbs.:
141-160 lbs.:
161-180 lbs.:
181-200 lbs.:
Over 201 lbs.:

Number of participants who are or use a:
Ambulatory:
Wheelchair:
Walker:
Cane:

Number of riding participants whose highest level is:
Walk on Lead:
Walk Ind.:
Trot on Lead:
Trot Ind:
Canter on Longe:
Canter Ind.:

Number who participate in:
Driving:
Ground Lessons:
Hippotherapy:
Riding:
Vaulting:
Other:

Number whose primary disability is:
Addiction:
Alcoholism:
Amputee:
Autism Spectrum:
Bipolarism:
Chromosomal:
Cerebral Palsy:
Depression:
Development Delay:
Down Syndrome:
Dwarfism:
Emotional:
Fetal Alcohol Synd.:
Hearing Impaired:
Learning Disability:
Mental Illness (other):
Muscular Sclerosis:
PTSD:
Speech/Lang. Delay:
Stroke:
Tourette Syndrome:
Traumatic Brain Injury:
Vision Impaired:
Other:

Number of participants who can:
Groom a horse:
Lead a horse:
Mount independently:
Post the trot:
Know their diagonal:
Catch a horse:
Feed a horse:
Tack a horse:

Appendix C: Program Horse Statistics

For a downloadable copy of this form, please go to:
lisawysocky.com/therapyhorseselectionforms

Therapy Horse Selection: Program Horse Statistics

	Horse 1	Horse 2	Horse 3	Horse 4	Horse 5
Basic Information					
Year of Birth					
Current Age					
Arrival Date					
Breed					
Color					
Markings					
Height					
Weight					
Barrel Width					
Chest Width					
Sex					
Temperament					
Background					
Program					
Rider Weight Limit					
Staff Weight Limit					
Movement at Walk					
Movement at Trot/Gait					
Movement at Canter					
Ease of Transitions					
Tracks Up/Overtracks					
Skills in Lessons					
Walk on Lead					
Trot on Lead					
Independent Walk					
Independent Trot					
Independent Canter					
Turn on Forehand					
Turn on Hindquarters					
Shoulder In/Out					
Sidepasses					
Longe Line Lesson					
Ground Drives					
Drives					
Vaulting					
Hippotherapy					

Appendix D: Horse Donation Form

For a downloadable copy of this form, please go to:
lisawysocky.com/therapyhorseselectionforms

Therapy Horse Selection: Horse Donation Form

Owner Name: ________________________ Email address: ____________________________
Owner Address: ____
Home Phone: _________________________ Cell Phone: ______________________________
Address where horse lives: ____
Horse's Name: ___________________ Breed: _______________________ Registered? ❑ Y ❑ N
Age: _____ Sex: ____ Color: ____________ Height: ______ Markings: _________________
Blemishes/Scars (if any) : ____
How long have you owned the horse? ______ Previous Use: ______________________________
Please rate your horse on a scale of 1 (calm) to 5 (spirited): ________ Is your horse gaited? ❑ Y ❑ N
Does your horse: ❑ Canter under saddle? ❑ Sidepass ❑ Collect/Extend ❑ Do trail obstacles
Please describe any awards your horse has won: _____________________________________
Does your horse: ❑ Crib ❑ Weave ❑ Cross Tie ❑ Drive ❑ Longe ❑ Trail Ride ❑ Trailer Load
In the pasture, is your horse: ❑ Dominant ❑ Submissive ❑ In the Middle
Has your horse ever choked, been ill, or diagnosed with Cushings or Metabolic Disorder? ❑ Y ❑ N
If yes, please describe: ____
Was your horse ever lame? ❑ Abscess ❑ Laminitis/Founder ❑ Navicular ❑ Hocks Injected ❑ Other
If yes, please describe: ____
Does your horse need special shoeing? ❑ Y ❑ N
If yes, please describe: ____
Does your horse have allergies, heaves, persistent cough, or other chronic conditions? ❑ Y ❑ N
If yes, please describe: ____
List amount of horse's feed and product fed: ____
Is your horse on pasture: ❑ Y ❑ N If yes, how many hours a day? ____________
Is your horse on any supplements or medication? ❑ Y ❑ N
If yes, please describe: ____
Please attach photos of the horse's: ❑ Head ❑ Side/Profile ❑ Front/Back Ends ❑ Being Ridden
Why will your horse make a good therapy horse? _____________________________________

Veterinarian Name: _______________________________ Phone: __________________________
Farrier/Trimmer Name: _____________________________ Phone: __________________________
May we call your veterinarian? ❑ Y ❑ N May we call your farrier/trimmer? ❑ Y ❑ N
Please attach recent medical records, or list the most recent dates for:
Coggins: _______ EWT/Encephalitis: ______ Rabies: _______ Rhino/flu: ______ West Nile: ________
Other: ____________________ Worming: ______ Worming Product: _______________________

OFFICE USE: Date Profile Received: _________ Phone Interview: ________ Horse Visit: __________
Staff/Equine Team Review: ______ Approved for trial? ❑ Y ❑ N Date owner notified Y or N: _______
If N, reasons: ____

Appendix E: Horse Assessment Form

For a downloadable copy of this form, please go to:
lisawysocky.com/therapyhorseselectionforms

Horse Assessment Form (page 1 of 2)

Evaluated By: Date:
Horse's Name:

Evaluate each skill, then calculate score at bottom.
Scoring: 1 - 5 (1 = Not performed; 5 = perfect); NE = Not Evaluated, NA = Not Applicable

	Skill - Feel free to make notes if needed.	Score
	Unmounted:	
1	Stands to be caught and haltered in the pasture	
2	Walks easily through gate(s) and into barn	
3	Walks calmly to grooming/tacking area, ties well, and stands nicely	
4	Stays quiet during: ❑ Loud Noises (doors shutting, feet stomping), ❑ Activity (quick moves, people/horses walking by) ❑ Nerf Toy ❑ Balls ❑ Bells ❑ Other ________	
5	Walks and turns easily with leader in correct position	
6	Trots easily and maintains trot until asked to walk	
7	Backs: 3-5 steps from ground with halter cues	
8	Accepts sidewalkers: ❑ One Sidewalker ❑ Two Sidewalkers	
	Mounted: Independent Riding	
9	Is easily: ❑ Saddled ❑ Bridled	
10	Stands quietly to be mounted from a block	
11	Walk: Easily changes direction, turns and bends well	
12	Trot: Picks up easily and smoothly, comes back to walk smoothly	
13	Trot: Does serpentines and changes directions well	
14	Sitting trot: ❑ Consistent Rhythm ❑ Smooth ❑ Choppy ❑ Bouncy ❑ Other ________	
15	Posting trot: ❑ Consistent Rhythm	
16	Canter: Picks up correctly and easily from trot ❑ Left Lead ❑ Right Lead	
17	Canter: Picks up correctly and easily from walk ❑ Left Lead ❑ Right Lead	
18	Canter: Downward transitions are smooth: ❑ To Trot ❑ To Walk	
19	Backs: 3-5 steps without resistance	
20	Open Riding: Quietly walks/trots outside of riding ring or on trail	
21	Moves both toward and away from barn area easily	
	Mounted: Lesson Simulation	
22	Calm during rider movements: ❑ Leaning ❑ Leg scissors ❑ Touching Mane and Tail	
23	Is quiet for: ❑ Nerf Toys ❑ Balls ❑ Plastic ❑ Other ________	
24	Remains calm and relaxed for: ❑ Bells ❑ Other Noisemakers	
25	Accepts sidewalker(s) at walk: ❑ One Sidewalker ❑ Two Sidewalkers	
26	Accepts sidewalker(s) at trot: ❑ One Sidewalker ❑ Two Sidewalkers	
27	Is quiet when rider makes loud noises	
28	Responds to leader if given cues from both leader and rider	
29	Walks and turns easily with leader in correct position	
30	Trots easily when led with a rider and maintains trot until asked to walk	
31	Stands quietly to be dismounted	
	TOTAL	

SCORE: ____________ divided by ____________ X 100 = ______ %

Total divided by Total Points Available* X 100 = %

*To calculate Total Points Available: Add the number of skills scored, then multiply by 5.

Appendix E: Horse Assessment Form, continued

HORSE ASSESSMENT FORM (PAGE 2 OF 2)

Horse's Name:

Tracking: ❑ Undertracks ❑ Tracks Up ❑ Overtracks ❑ Tracks Evenly Left and Right
❑ Tracks Straight From Behind Comments:

Tail Carriage: ❑ Flat ❑ Left ❑ Right ❑ Clamped ❑ Outward

Posture: ❑ Shoulders Hunched ❑ Tail Clamped ❑ Tight Walk ❑ Low Neck ❑ Pinned Ears

Soreness: ❑ Yes ❑ No Where: ____

Disposition: ❑ Poll Drop ❑ Disengages Hips ❑ Friendly ❑ Distant ❑ Pushy
Comments:

Conformation: ❑ Square ❑ Rectangle ❑ Tall Rectangle ❑ Level Hips ❑ Eyes Wide Set
Comments:

Flexing: ❑ Nose to Chest ❑ Nose to Girth Left ❑ Nose to Girth Right ❑ Leg Stretches
Comments:

Movement: Walk is: ❑ Front to Back ❑ Side to Side ❑ Rotational
Trot is: ❑ Flat ❑ Elevated ❑ Choppy ❑ Uneven ❑ Smooth
Comments:

How would this horse fit into our program?:

Additional Comments:

Recommend for ninety-day trial? ❑ Yes ❑ No

Appendix F: The Ten-Minute Assessment

This quick, ten-minute assessment will help you quickly evaluate horses who might end up in your personal barn, or at your local program. It will take some time, but with enough practice you can learn to spot and evaluate many of the items below in mere seconds.

PHYSICAL SOUNDNESS

Horse's Body Shape—is the body square, tall, or rectangular? Different body shapes give different movement, and long, rectangular horses have long backs that can limit the amount of weight the horse carries.

Eyes Set Wide—horses who have eyes set widely have a better range of vision and, as a whole, tend to be less spooky.

Neck Bend—can the horse flex his or her nose back to the girth area? Is flexion equal on both sides? Limited or unequal flexion can be a sign of arthritis or needed chiropractic work.

Poll Drop—does the horse drop his head when you touch the poll or pull down on the halter? A drop indicates submissiveness and trust. No drop indicates the horse is a herd leader or mistrustful.

Flank Touch—does the horse move his or her hips away when you touch the barrel or flank? Is the movement even on the left and right sides? No movement can indicate soreness or arthritis, or a very dominant horse.

Hips Level—are the horse's hips level? Uneven hips can mean arthritis, chronic unsoundness, or that chiropractic work is needed.

Tail Centered—does the horse carry the top part of his or her tail centered between the butt cheeks? A tail carried to the left or right can mean general soreness, or even serious lower back or hip problems.

General Soreness—when you run your hands over the horse's body, does the horse pin his or her ears? If so, the horse could be bad tempered, or have a lot of soreness.

Travels Evenly—when you watch the horse walk, does he or she track evenly front to back and left to right? If not, arthritis or chronic soreness might be an issue.

Mental Strength—does the horse seem level headed and sensible, especially in unusual situations?

Demeanor—what is the horse's general demeanor? Quiet, anxious, pushy, or . . .? First impressions are usually correct.

Flinching—does the horse flinch when you toss a small towel against his sides or flanks? Is the reaction the same on both sides? Lots of flinching can mean a nervous or insecure horse. Be sure to keep your body language neutral so the horse does not pick up on an expectation of excitement.

Plastic Bag—after careful introduction, when you toss a plastic bag against the horse is the flinching the same as with a towel, or increased?

Soft Toy—after introduction, can you toss a soft toy against the horse's neck or barrel with little or no reaction? Can you toss it under the barrel, or in front of or behind the horse? This is a good test of the horse's possible reaction if something unusual happens during a lesson.

Nerf Ball—can you roll a nerf or other small ball around the horse's body with little to no reaction? Again, a good test of the horse's reaction to the unexpected.

Sidewalkers—does the horse calmly accept first one sidewalker, and then two when the horse is unmounted? Or, does he pin his ears, refuse to move forward, or cow kick? This tests the horse's issue of personal space. In many EAAT activities there are multiple people close to the horse.

Whorl—this old superstition may have merit! What direction the whorl(s) on the forehead go, where they are, and the number of them may predict a horse's disposition and personality.

MOUNTED ASSESSMENT

Owner Ride—how does the horse behave when his or her current owner rides? Does the horse track up and travel much as he did without a rider, or are there significant differences? Also look at the tail carriage. Flat, or off to the left or right?

Body Lean—does the horse come up underneath the rider when the rider leans to the left, right, front, or back? Does the horse try to stop? These are signs that the horse is taking care of his or her rider, and that the horse is concerned about a rider who is unbalanced.

Leg Scissors—when you scissor your legs back and forth when riding, is the horse goosey? Does he jump forward or become impatient? If so, this might not be a good horse for beginners or tight-legged riders, such as those with cerebral palsy.

Arm Movements—how does the horse react when a rider is being led and brings her arms out to the side, overhead, in front, etcetera? If nervously, the horse may be timid, insecure, or not trust easily.

Noise—what happens when you make odd noises from the horse's back? Does the horse raise his or her head and neck much higher than normal? Does he or she try to scoot forward?

Sidewalkers—How does the horse respond to first one sidewalker when being led with a rider, and then with two sidewalkers? Horses who have problems with sidewalkers typically have personal space issues that cannot be overcome.

Gaits—how do the horse's gaits feel under saddle? Is the walk an even four-beat gait? What direction does the walk move the rider's pelvis? Is the trot choppy, big, or smooth? Is the horse forward or lazy under saddle?

Supplemental Resources

The following titles are highly recommended for supplemental reading and viewing:

Almost a Whisper
by Sam Powell

Beyond the 9 Points of Saddle Fitting (DVD)
by Jochen Schleese

Getting in TTouch: Understand and Influence Your Horse's Personality
by Linda Tellington-Jones

Horse Health Care
by Cherry Hill and Richard Klimesh

My Horse My Partner: Teamwork on the Ground
by Lisa Wysocky (also available in DVD format)

Suffering in Silence: The Saddle-Fit Link to Physical and Psychological Trauma in Horses
by Jochen Schleese

The Horse Conformation Handbook
by Heather Smith Thomas

The Revolution in Horsemanship
by Dr. Robert Miller and Rick Lamb

Glossary

The following terms are used to describe various aspects of horses, their tack, and equipment. While many more terms could have been included, this glossary has been limited to those that might come into play when looking for a new horse. In some cases, a word has several meanings, but only those meanings most relevant to the horse selection process have been included. Some terms are quite basic, but are included for those readers who are new to horses or to equine assisted therapies and activities, or to further explain use of the word earlier in the book.

Action: The amount a horse elevates his or her legs, knees, hocks, and feet.

Aged Horse: An older horse. Sometimes referred to as a horse with a "smooth mouth." In horse racing and in some horse shows, an aged horse is one over four years of age.

Aids: Cues from the rider, driver, or handler that ask the horse for a response. Generally broken into two categories: natural and artificial. Natural aids include hands, seat, weight, legs, and voice. Artificial aids extend, reinforce, or substitute natural aids and include bits, whips, spurs, and martingales.

Ankle: Incorrect term for the fetlock joint, as the hock most closely corresponds to the human ankle.

Balk: When a horse refuses to move.

Barefoot: When a horse does not wear horseshoes.

Bell boot: A type of protective boot worn by a horse.

Blowing: A sound made by a horse who sharply exhales through flared nostrils. A horse might blow when curious, meeting another horse, or shying away from an object, or to clear sinus cavities to inhale scent.

Bolting: When a horse suddenly runs away (with or without a rider).

Bone: Used to describe the quality of the horse's skeletal structure. Also refers to the size and density of bone of the lower leg, which helps determine the amount of weight the horse can carry.

Bosal: A type of noseband used on hackamore horses of the vaquero tradition. Usually made of braided rawhide, it is fitted to allow it to rest quietly until the rider uses the reins to give a signal. It acts upon the horse's nose and jaw.

Botfly, bot: A parasitic fly that lays eggs on the legs, face, and shoulders of horses. The tiny, yellow eggs are licked by the horse and, when ingested, hatch into maggots, called bots, which attach to the horse's stomach lining.

Bowed tendon: An enlarged tendon along the back of the cannon bone that often is caused by heavy work.

Breeching: A wide strap around the rear of a horse to hold a saddle in place, or allow a harnessed horse to pull back on the shafts or pole of a vehicle to slow it.

Breedy: A horse who conforms to breed type. Also used to describe horses of thinner build, such as a Thoroughbred or Arabian.

Bridging: When the center of the side of a saddle pulls away from a horse's body.

Bucking: A behavior where the horse lowers his head and rapidly kicks his hind feet into the air. At liberty, a buck is seen as an expression of energy or high spirit. Under saddle it is considered a disobedience.

Bute: Common term for Phenylbutazone, a non-steroid anti-inflammatory drug (NSAID) used to control pain and swelling in horses.

By: The relationship of a horse to her sire in the context of pedigree. A foal is by his sire and out of his dam.

Cannon bone: The third metacarpal or metatarsal bone of the lower leg. Sometimes called the shin bone, but it is actually comparable to bones in the human palm or foot. In horses it is a large bone and provides support for the body weight of the horse.

Canter: A three-beat gait. In western disciplines, the canter is known as a lope. The order in which the feet hit the ground depends on which front leg leads, but the gait begins with the outside hind, followed by both the inside hind outside front together, then the inside front. There is a moment during a canter when all four hooves are off the ground, known as the moment of suspension.

Capped Elbow: A swelling of the bursa caused by injury.

Capped Hock: *See Capped Elbow.*

Carriage: A two- or four-wheeled vehicle drawn by horses and used for carrying people. Also the way a horse will carry himself, especially in the positioning of the head, neck, and hocks.

Cart: A two-wheeled vehicle pulled by one or more horses.

Chestnuts: A callous on the inside of the leg above the knee on the foreleg, and below the hock on the hind leg. Chestnuts vary in size and shape and are sometimes compared to fingerprints in humans. For purposes of identification, some breed registries require photographs of a horse's chestnuts, among other individual characteristics.

Choke: A blockage of the esophagus, most often linked to a horse eating too fast. A horse who is choking can breathe, but not eat or drink.

Chrome: Slang for eye-catching white markings on a horse, usually stockings or socks. Also used to refer to flashy Paint, Pinto, or Appaloosa markings.

Cinch: A wide, flat girth of mohair, reinforced felt, or an equivalent synthetic material used with a strap to secure a western saddle to the back of a horse. Some western saddles have a front cinch and a looser back cinch.

Coach: A carriage, usually closed and drawn by two or more horses.

Colic: Any number of painful digestive disorders, usually characterized by intestinal displacement or blockage. Colic is a leading cause of equine death.

Conformation: The shape and proportion of a horse's body.

Coronet Band: The ring of soft tissue just above the hoof that blends into the skin of the leg.

Coupling: The sunken area on the horse's side below the lumbar vertebrae, behind the last rib, and in front of the point of the hip. Ideally should be as short as possible.

Crest: The top of the horse's neck, from poll to wither.

Cribbing: A vice where the horse grabs the edge of an object, such as a fence board, with his incisor teeth and sucks in air. Sucking air without grasping anything with the teeth is called windsucking.

Croup: The topline and underlying musculature of the hindquarters. The croup runs from the tail to the loin, and from the point of the hip to the point of the buttock.

Crowhop: A mild form of bucking consisting of a stiff-legged hop with a rounded back. Does not involve kicking up the back legs.

Curb: A blemish in the hock area that can cause lameness. Also, any number of soft tissue injuries of the hock area.

Diagonal: At a trot, the set of legs that move forward at the same time are the "diagonal" pair. Also, when a rider posts the trot, he can rise either when the left or the right foreleg and opposite hind leg come forward. If he rises when the left foreleg comes forward, he is on the left diagonal. (When riding a clockwise circle, the rider rises when the outside front and inside hind legs come forward.) In dressage or driving competitions, a diagonal is a line that crosses the center of the ring from one corner to the other.

Dock: The muscular portion of a horse's tail, where the hair is rooted. Sometimes refers only to the upper portion of this area, where the tail attaches to the hindquarters. Also, to cut a horse's tail at the dock, seen most often on carriage and draft horses to keep their tails from becoming caught in the harness.

Draft Horse: Generic term for many breeds of large, muscular, heavy horses developed primarily as farm or harness horses who plow fields, pull wagons, log timber, and do other, similar, heavy pulling work.

Dressage: A classical, slow form of training that involves mastering levels.

Driving: Guiding and controlling one or more horses from behind, such as from a horse-drawn vehicle, or from the ground. Guidance is by long reins and voice.

Easy Keeper: A horse who needs little food to maintain condition and who may be prone to obesity.

Equine: Any member of the genus Equus.

Equitation: The skill of riding a horse. Also, a term for horse show events that are judged on the rider's ability instead of that of the horse.

Equus: The genus that includes the horse, donkey, zebra and all other members of the Equidae family.

Ergot: A small callus on the back of the fetlock, often concealed by hair and thought to be a remnant of the pad of the prehistoric toe.

Farrier: A professional hoof care specialist who does hoof trimming and who also uses blacksmithing skills to shoe horses.

Feathers: Long hair on the fetlocks. Most horses have some feathers, but in draft breeds it may cover the feet and extend well up the leg. Many people trim the feathers off, but they serve to wick water away from the hoof.

Fetlock: The joint above the pastern. It is equivalent to the base joint of a human finger or toe.

Filly: A young female horse, normally under four years of age.

Flank: The very upper portion of a horse's back leg behind the barrel.

Float: To rasp down sharp points that form on equine teeth. Usually performed by a veterinarian or equine dentistry specialist.

Founder: The most severe form of laminitis, an inflammatory condition that affects the laminae of the hoof. The third phalanx (the coffin bone) rotates, often becomes deformed, and in severe cases, may puncture the bottom surface of the hoof. It is a leading cause of death among horses, especially in breeds that are easy keepers.

Frog: A tough, rubbery, triangular part of the underside of a horse hoof that acts as a shock absorber for the foot and assists in blood circulation of the lower leg.

Gallop: The fastest natural gait. Like the canter, there is a moment during a gallop when all four hooves are off the ground, known as the moment of suspension. At fastest speeds, the gallop differs from the canter in that it becomes an irregular four-beat gait, rather than a three-beat gait. Where diagonal front and hind legs hit the ground simultaneously in the canter, the step is broken into two beats that follow each other in very quick succession in the gallop.

Gait: The sequence in which a horse moves its legs is a gait. Gaits are divided into natural gaits (those performed by most horses), and those that are either trained by humans, or are specific to a few breeds. The natural gaits are walk, trot, canter/lope, and gallop. Other gaits include the pace, and ambling gaits such as the rack and running walk.

Gaited Horse: A horse who performs an ambling gait other than, or in addition to, the trot. Many breeds are considered gaited, including the Peruvian Paso, Paso Fino, Saddlebred, Missouri Fox Trotter, and Tennessee Walking Horse.

Girth: A wide, flat strap made of leather, canvas, cord, or similar synthetic material with buckles at each end, used in conjunction with the saddle's billets to secure an English saddle to a horse's back.

Goosey: Overly sensitive to leg cues; jumpy.

Grade: A horse who has only a small amount of recognizable breeding, or none at all. Generally unregistered and unregisterable.

Green: A horse or rider who is either untrained or has just started training.

Green-broke: A horse who has just begun training and is inexperienced.

Groundwork: To train or exercise a horse without a rider from the ground.

Hackamore: A type of headgear that uses a noseband or a bosal for control instead of a bit.

Hand: A measurement of the height of a horse. Originally taken from the size of a grown man's hand but now standardized to four inches. The measurement is taken from the ground to the withers. It is expressed with a number, a period and a second number. 15.3 hands would be fifteen times four inches, plus three inches, or 63 inches.

Hand Gallop: A controlled gallop, with a speed between that of a canter and a full gallop. Derives from the idea that the gallop is under the control of the rider's hand.

Hard Keeper: A horse who needs a large amount of food to maintain condition.

Harness: Tack placed on a horse to hitch him to a cart, plow, wagon or other horse-drawn vehicle.

Head-shy: A horse who is hesitant to have his head or ears touched.

Head Stall: The portion of the bridle that goes over the horse's ears and holds the bit in place.

Heavy: A rider who uses too much rein pressure is said to have heavy hands. Or, in racing, a track that is between muddy and good (one that is drying out) is called heavy. Also, a draft horse is sometimes called a heavy horse.

Hinny: The hybrid offspring of a female donkey and a male horse. The hybrid with the reverse parentage (and somewhat different appearance and characteristics) is a mule.

Hock: A joint of the horse's hind leg, midway between the body and the ground. The hock corresponds to the ankle and heel of the human.

Jack: An uncastrated male donkey or ass.

Jennet: A small, gaited horse developed in Spain, used as a riding animal. Or, a female donkey.

Jenny: A female donkey, sometimes called a jennet.

Jog: A slow trot most often seen in western riding.

Knee: The joint of a horse's front leg between the cannon and the forearm. It is equivalent to the human wrist.

Laminitis: Inflammation of the laminae of the hoof, and linked to Metabolic syndrome (Cushings), obesity, or ingestion of excess starches or sugars. Laminitis can cause lameness and severe pain.

Lead: The leading front leg of the horse at the canter and gallop. On a curve, a horse is generally asked to lead with the inside leg. Also a lead rope, a flat line or rope attached to a halter to lead the animal when the handler is on the ground.

Leader: The person who leads the horse in a therapeutic lesson or session.

Longe: To train a horse at the end of a long rope or line. Typically, the horse moves at different gaits in a large circle around his human partner.

Long Driving: Driving a horse with very long reins while walking behind. Used for training, both for riding and driving. Also called long lining or long reining.

Lope: A form of slow canter seen in western-style riding.

Markings: The white markings on the horse's face, legs, and the odd white body spot.

Martingale: A piece of tack used to control head carriage, used in both riding and driving.

Mechanical hackamore: A bitless headgear where the reins connect to shanks placed between a noseband and a curb chain.

Mule: The hybrid offspring of a male donkey and a female horse. Mules are almost always sterile. The hybrid with the reverse parentage (and somewhat different appearance and characteristics) is a hinny.

Near Side: The left side of a horse, which is the traditional side where activities around a horse are traditionally done.

Neck Rein: The act of turning a horse by touching the reins to the side of the horse's neck. The horse turns away from the rein pressure. Useful when riding one-handed.

Off: A term used when a horse is lame or unsound.

Off Side: The right-hand side of a horse.

On the Bit: A horse who is flexed at the poll, balanced, moving forward well, and responsive to the rider.

On the Buckle: In English riding, holding the reins very loose, by the buckle that joins the reins together.

Out of: The relationship of a horse to his mother in the context of his pedigree. A foal is by his sire and out of his dam.

Pace: A two-beat, lateral gait where the front and hind legs on the same side move forward at the same time.

Parrot Mouth: A malformation of the jaw where the upper incisor teeth protrude beyond the lower jaw. A severe parrot mouth could make chewing difficult for the horse, as it is a major equine overbite.

Pastern: The part of the leg between the fetlock and the coronary band.

Pointing: Resting a foreleg in indication of soreness in that leg or foot.

Pony: In general, small horses who mature shorter than 14.2 hands, or 58 inches. Also, to lead one horse while riding another.

Purebred: An animal with documented parentage recognized by a breed registry and free of breeding from lines outside those of the breed in question. Not to be confused with Thoroughbred, which is a specific breed of horse.

Rearing: When a horse rises up on his hind legs.

Sand Roll: An area covered with deep sand, used by horses to roll in.

Shying: When a horse jumps in fright, usually at a sudden movement or an unfamiliar object.

Side Reins: Tack that runs from the bit to the saddle or surcingle and used to develop flexion, balance, and softness. Can easily be used incorrectly, so is best used by an experienced trainer.

Sidewalker: A support person who walks to the side of the rider during the lesson or session. Sometimes there will be two sidewalkers, one on each side, who provide physical, emotional, or cognitive support for the rider.

Smooth Mouth: Older horses who have worn the indentations or "cups" from their incisors, which can occur about the age of eight.

Sound: Terminology used to describe a healthy horse.

Sour: A horse who is grumpy and unhappy when being worked with.

Splint: Ossification of small bones on the inside of the cannon bone. Splints are hard bumps that often form after trauma. An unsoundness when newly injured, a splint may mature into a blemish with no effect on soundness.

Sport Horse: General term for a horse bred and/or trained for eventing, dressage, and jumping. May also include hunters and horses trained for combined driving.

Stock Horse: A horse who herds livestock, or is trained for reining, roping or cutting; a generic term for breeds developed for handling cattle. Also used to describe the Appaloosa, Quarter Horse, and Paint breeds.

Stocky: A short, squat horse with bunchy muscles.

Stride: The distance from the imprint of a forefoot until the same foot hits the ground again; one cycle of movement of all four of the horse's legs.

Stringhalt: A disorder that causes a jerking movement and a higher than the natural gait of one or both hind legs.

Substance: Assessment of the overall muscularity of a horse, width and depth of body, and quality of bone.

Surcingle: Equipment that goes around the barrel of the horse. It often has rings at various locations for attachment of reins.

Tack: A generic term for horse equipment.

Therapy Horse: A horse who assists humans in physical, cognitive, and/or emotional growth.

Thigh Hold: A supportive hold where the fingers of the sidewalker's hand that are next to the horse tuck under the saddle and the arm drapes across the rider's thigh.

Topline: The area on a horse that runs from the poll to the dock of the tail; on a pedigree chart, the paternal side of the ancestry, which is found on the top of the chart.

Transition: The change from one gait to another.

Trimmer: One who trims horse's feet, but who typically does not shoe horses.

Typey: Slang for a horse who conforms to his breed standards or type.

Unsound: A horse with significant lameness or other health problems.

Vice: A habit that makes the horse difficult to work with, such as biting, kicking, bucking, cribbing, weaving, etcetera.

Warmblood: A descriptive word for many middle-weight sport horse breeds. Most originated in Europe by crossbreeding draft horses with light breeds such as the Thoroughbred or Arabian. "Warm" refers to the cross of a cold-blood and a hot-blood. It does not relate to body temperature.

Weaving: A habit developed by some horses who are kept for long periods in a stall, where the horse repetitively sways side to side, shifting weight and moving his head and neck back and forth.

Wind Puff: A puffy bump filled with excess synovial fluid. Usually seen on the fetlock joint; also sometimes seen on the knee. Wind puffs are caused by injury or overuse, but rarely cause lameness.

Whorl: A circular arrangement of hairs, usually on a horse's forehead, neck or chest. Their location is one means of horse identification, and may indicate personality.

PHOTO CREDITS

Cover:

Tessie (Quarter Horse/Belgian cross) photo by Lisa Wysocky

Baby (Tennessee Walking Horse cross) photo by Lisa Wysocky

T-Ball (Fjord) photo courtesy Central Kentucky Riding for Hope, Lexington, Kentucky

Interior:

All photos by or courtesy of Lisa Wysocky, unless otherwise noted.

ABOUT THE AUTHOR

Award-winning author, trainer, and instructor, Lisa Wysocky combines a career of books and horses. Lisa's fun, debut horse mystery, *The Opium Equation*, received four prestigious awards and rave reviews, and the sequel, *The Magnum Equation*, was chosen as Best Equine-related Book of 2013 at the American Horse Publications Awards. Lisa also co-authored *Front of the Class*, which aired as a Hallmark Hall of Fame movie. She is co-author of *Walking on Eggshells* with Lyssa Chapman, a star of the A&E reality program *Dog the Bounty Hunter*; and *Hidden Girl,* written with Shyima Hall, which won the Junior Library Guild Award. Lisa is a PATH instructor, mentor, and ESMHL who educates horses for therapeutic riding and other equine assisted activities, and has been chosen by the American Riding Instructors Association as one of the Top 50 riding instructors in the nation. She lives in Tennessee and Minnesota and supports ColbysArmy.org. To learn more, go to: LisaWysocky.com. Please also follow Lisa on Twitter at @LisaWysocky, and on her horse Facebook site that she shares with horseman Sam Powell at: facebook.com/thepowerofawhisper. She thanks ACTHA (actha.us), and Wrangler/VF Jeanswear.

IF YOU LIKED THIS BOOK YOU MAY ALSO LIKE OTHER BOOKS BY LISA WYSOCKY

The Opium Equation: A Cat Enright Equestrian Mystery

Winner: Mom's Choice Awards, American Horse Publications Awards, IBPA Awards, National Indie Excellence Awards

When retired movie star Glenda Dupree was murdered in her antebellum mansion in Tennessee, there was much speculation. Prior to leaving life on earth, Glenda had offended everyone, including her neighbor, a (mostly) law-abiding horse trainer named Cat Enright. Cat finds Glenda's body, is implicated in the murder, and also in the disappearance of a ten-year-old neighbor, Bubba Henley. An unpopular sheriff and upcoming election mean the pressure to close the case is on. With the help of her riding students, a (possibly) psychic horse, a local cop, a kid named Frog, and an eccentric client of a certain age with electric blue hair, Cat takes time from her horse training business to try to solve the case and keep herself out of prison.

The Magnum Equation: A Cat Enright Equestrian Mystery

Winner: American Horse Publications Awards

A horse trainer, juvenile delinquent, eccentric client of a certain age with electric blue hair, and a (possibly) psychic horse lead this Southern equestrian mystery into a fast paced, lightly comic read. Join Cat Enright and her crew as she tries to solve murder and mayhem at a prestigious all-breed horse show. When horses become ill and a show-goer's last hurrah is in the port-a-potty, Cat decides to find the cause of the trouble. Contains a reader guide, glossary, and recipe.

My Horse, My Partner: Teamwork on the Ground

This easy-to-follow guide provides training to create a steady, reliable horse that respects and trusts his handler. Using a method that she developed while training show horses, then refined training therapeutic riding horses, longtime horse trainer Lisa Wysocky shows how to use a toolkit of every-day items—such as halters, lead ropes, long lines, plastic bags, toys, towels, and voice commands—along with a variety of specialized ground exercises, to desensitize and build confidence with horses of all types and in all disciplines. The result is an unflappable horse that quietly accepts sudden or loud noises and unusual objects and/or situations. Illustrated with black-and-white photos throughout this beautifully designed hard cover book, *My Horse, My Partner* helps horse and human forge an amazing bond as they go through this process together.

Horse Country: A Celebration of Country Music and the Love of Horses

The perfect gift for anyone who loves horses and country music, this four-color hardcover coffee table book features twenty-seven stars of country music talking about their love of horses. Many never-seen-before color photos of the stars and their horses complete the heartwarming stories in the book.

For additional books and for other resources by Lisa Wysocky, please go to LisaWysocky.com